Reflections

of a

Radical Servant Leader

Courage to Let Your Life Speak

LORETTA B. RANDLE, M.A.

ISBN 978-1-63844-039-0 (paperback)
ISBN 978-1-63844-040-6 (digital)

Christian Faith Publishing
832 Park Avenue
Meadville, PA 16335
www.christianfaithpublishing.com

Printed in the United States of America

To my parents, Willie and Matteel Randle; my paternal grandparents (whom I never met), Willie Randle Sr. and Mae Lizza; my maternal grandparents, Robert "Bobby" and Gertrude Brown; my maternal great-grandmother, Sophia Byas; my still-living maternal 105-year-old great-aunt Eva Lee Addison-Whitt; and my paternal 106-year-old aunt Beatrice Randle-Phenix and in remembrance of the footprints between and across continents of the vibrant autobiographical storytelling and poetic mentoring of author-actress Maya Angelou

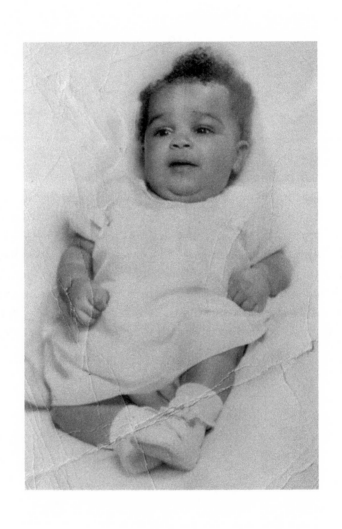

Contents

Preface

My Makeover

> You are witnesses declares the Lord, and my servant whom
> I have chosen, so that you may know and believe Me.
> —Isaiah 43:10

This book is about my journey of change and the transformation of my entangled human heart. It reveals how God apprehends an angry, emotionally damaged, militant-minded Black woman and single mother and begins the makeover of hard, harsh, and horrific tests, turning each one into a testimony. Through this process, a much better version of myself has emerged, bringing forth an incredibly kinder, gentler radical servant leader. When Jesus Christ comes into the life of a woman, she becomes bodacious and brave. Now that's radical!

Before I begin my makeover story, it is important to pay homage and acknowledge my African ancestry. I give thanks with a grateful heart to the generations of radical servant leaders of men, women, and children who died and survived the Middle Passage of the transatlantic slave trade and those who were forced into servitude (slavery) to tend the lands of the new frontiers of North and South America, Caribbean Islands, Europe, the Netherlands, Sweden, and other countries. My heart believes that God can and will use all things to transform humanity into the likeness of Christ. After all, God's word affirms, "Before I formed you in the womb, I knew you" (Jer. 1:5). Now that's radical!

What brings me to write on the topic of servant leadership? It would be my entry into seminary, at age sixty-two, that inspired and groomed my thoughts to contextualize my life experiences and events through the lens of servant leadership, a modern-day term coined by Robert Greenleaf. My professor affirmed my writing skills by encouraging me to take my thesis project theme and write my first book. Never in my life had I heard of such a thing. Me, a writer! I became tickled at the idea and accepted the challenge. Yet the act and art of writing remains tedious and no less easier. This book-writing effort has been five years in the making.

As a young girl growing up in small town Vallejo, California, it would be the radical servant leadership of my parents that set the path of service for me to follow. My father served in the United States Army as a cook during World War II. On rare occasions, he would share his culinary exploits with his family. My parents modeled strong work ethics before all ten of their children, in particular their eight girls. We were taught that service and work to humanity was in fact honoring God. Even accompanying my parents on their various domestic servant jobs was expected. My mother taught each of her girls to cook, clean, iron, and volunteer. By the age of ten, I knew the art and science of making homemade yeast rolls and how to iron my father's heavily starched khaki pants. Yet it would be my father who taught me how to scramble eggs without drying them out.

As early as age five, my sisters and I served in the church. Taylor Chapel CME Church is a small unassuming, well-manicured church building on the corner of Louisiana and Monterey Street in Vallejo, California. I recently learned it was Mother Mary Taylor and her three adult daughters who were moved by the Spirit in 1949 to mobilize, organize, and build a church. The doors of the church opened in 1953. It would be in this small church context that was organized and led by women where my servant leadership would be cultivated.

In the backdrop of all this servant character development was the encroaching heated and rising social tension of the civil rights movement of the 1960s led by Dr. Martin Luther King, Jr. and many others. The church, more specifically the black church, became the iconic radical servant leader—extending her hands by opening her doors, mobilizing peaceful protests, and more. Further, when I was a high school student, I recall the seed of service being planted even deeply in my soul. It was the words of former president John F. Kennedy. "Ask not what your country can do for you, but what you can do for your country." His assassination fueled my servant soul, which was already overfilled with anger.

Another major turning point in my makeover process came later in life. My servant's calling became radical and a bit militant after hearing a news report that an eighteen-month-old child had been sexually violated. It would be this event and other forces that propelled me to serve at-risk children and youth up close and personal. My mandate from the Holy Spirit was to open my heart and make covenant with vulnerable children and families through prayer and presence. What does it mean to be radical? I understand it to mean being incarnational, reaching down into the very root of something in order to change it—like Jesus. He lived, died, and was resurrected as a radical servant leader to the extreme, making you and me his priority in the process of transformation. What radical love.

It is my hope that this book will serve as inspiration, motivation, and innovation for believers, especially older adults, leading them to surrender places of grief and pain to the Lord of love who will transform them into something incomparably beloved.

After all, we are called to offer our lives as God's radical servant leaders for the cause of justice and the welfare of all children.

Introduction

The steps of a righteous man are ordered of the Lord...
—Psalm 37:23–25

What demands was God placing on my character? How did this older adult change from a militant-minded, angry African American caterpillar to a transformed and set-free butterfly? How did a book-writing endeavor emerge from the damaged soul of a daughter of the 1960s?

Some studies report that by 2030, baby boomers (older adults of fifty plus) will number nearly seventy million in the United States. Clearly, older adults are living longer although many are living in isolation. Others are discovering meaningful social engagements, and some are fully persuaded to practice the many and varied forms of physical fitness to stay useful. Older adults are reservoirs of untapped wisdom and servant-leader resources available to society.

Although Professional development visits to the former Soviet Union and missions' outreach to South Africa were under my belt, I had not fully heard nor committed my ways to serve God in specific foreign mission's field. Then at age sixty, God called me to make an intentional mission's decision to travel to Chennai, India, on an international Children In Prayer International consultation to meet with forty other nations of people who had hearts and calls to empower the voices of children to become prayer workers. I was in career transition, was unemployed, and was unsure about my fit in the kingdom of God.

In December 2007, I received a layoff notice that World Vision was shutting down its Los Angeles operations. In March of 2008, an invitation to join other child and youth advocate came from John Robb, former director of global prayer mobilization of World Vision International. World Vision is one of the oldest and largest Christian community development relief and child advocacy organizations in the world. It has a presence in over one hundred countries. At the time, my role was manager of vision youth initiative, a World Vision US community outreach program in Los Angeles, California. My heart and mind were being reconstituted to think differently and globally of unique and inventive ways to serve vulnerable children and families.

Without an income stream or definite vocational/career plans, I found myself on my way to Chennai, India, to meet up with other like-minded servants of God. My heart and mind were set aflame with divine intention to focus on equipping and developing children and youth to speak to God directly.

What happened to set my heart aflame? It was the incredible and profound ministry of Father Antonne of Royal Children's Ministry in India that ignited a burning to save and equipped the voices of our children with the Gospel of Salvation. It was during a foot washing and induction ceremony of new children into the ministry. Children who were labeled "untouchables" in India's caste system. Children who had been thrown away by overwhelmed parents and many other social determinants, who were left to fend for themselves on the streets—the least, last and lost. Yet, it would be the amazing grace and compassion of Father Antonne, founder of Royal Children's Ministry. His team included former "untouchables"; mostly young women who had been rescued by this ministry. They were serving now in leadership roles. Teams who search for and would gather up children from the streets, dumpsters and other sites. Father Antonne's team would clean them up, educate them and place them in servant leader roles on this innovative campus.

On stage during the foot washing ceremony, the children were in tears, and so was I. The atmosphere was pregnant with worship and praise singing and dancing by his team. It was in this moment;

Father Antonne extended an invitation to ministers and pastors in the audience to join him on stage and love on the children and wash their feet too. Holy Spirit moved on me to go up and hold one of these precious souls in my arms. It was a moving experience for me. The love of Christ for his little children shone brilliantly that evening.

Thus, Children's Prayer Initiative was conceived. On my return to the United States, I went into planning mode to organize and launch Children's Prayer Summit. In cooperation with Dr. Velma Union of One Light International and Apostle Juanda Green of New Visions Christian Fellowship, over thirty families responded to the call to bring their children and collectively participate in the 2008 Children's Prayer Summit. Twelve years since then, my home remains open to host a five-day children and youth enrichment and empowerment intensive.

When I reflect on Psalm 37:23–25, David shares how we are to practice wisdom over worry. Theologian David Guzik offers insight that is worth noting. He says, "David knew that among his ancestors there were some who left Israel, fearful in a time of great famine."[1] Naomi and her husband and sons left for Moab in search of a better outcome when they experienced great loss and devastation. Only Naomi and Ruth survived. Naomi's husband and two sons died. "When they returned after several disastrous years in Moab, they found the people of Bethlehem in Israel provided for. God knew how to take care of those who trusted in Him in times of famine, and has done so since then."[2]

In the midst of intense times of great emotional and social upheavals, the Lord taught me to trust Him to meet my every need. My spirit was being nurtured and wooed by the grace of God. Friends and family were inspired of the Lord to encourage me. Resources and care packages were often brought by or left on my porch by a few. My siblings helped with keeping my mortgage payments current, and my son (when I was not too proud to ask) would transfer funds into my personal account. I continued to pout and ponder, *Where had I missed the mark that put me in this financial predicament?*

It would take several years before I would yield and grasp the reality that self-effort was not my source; it was God. In David's reflections, he takes note that "God takes care of those who put their trust in Him and walk in His righteousness" (Ps 37:23–24). Today my belief and practice are more inclined to trust in God than self-effort and are fueled by ancient spiritual disciplines taught through contemplative prayer methods like breath prayer, centering prayer, and Lectio Divina. These practices were introduced to me during my first course in the Master of Arts in Global Urban Leadership program with Bakke Graduate University. Time alone with God in devotion, study, and practice of servant leadership frame how I move and have my being in God.

My mind and heart are slowly but steadily moving from a militant approach to changing the world to a soft-serve, servant-leader approach of changes that bring and nurture lasting changes. Servant leadership as a best practice is perceived by some as a passive approach to change. This approach was the total opposite of the way in which I was oriented to changing the world during the 1960s. Angry messages of change and challenges could be heard and seen by the people and by the government. The message of Black power was needed and, by whatever means, necessary. I was conflicted with this approach. Yet I was drawn to the Black nationalist message of Black ownership in every aspect of life: raise and teach our children in the collective community, business ownership, and more. It was the most aggressive method of change in which some militant-minded African American people were willing to engage. Yet it was the redemptive freedom song by the Beattle's, "Give Love a Chance," that resonated deep within my soul. Dr. Martin Luther King Jr. and the civil rights movement were leaving an incredible and unforgettable footprint of nonviolent protest for justice, peace, and love on my heart and on the landscape of America to change its laws and heart toward its treatment of African Americans and poor people, past and present, and to work toward achieving justice for all oppressed people.

After my mission trip to Chennai, India, in 2008, I knew God was up to something pretty amazing in my life. I had to find a way to get still, quiet, and prayerful. What my eyes beheld and my ears heard in India created space and opportunity for the Lord to plant a seed of social-justice action for vulnerable children from a global perspective. My eyes beheld His Glory fill the stage. The love of Christ Presence came upon the children, upon me. Never had I experienced such love, nor seen Christ show up and pursue his children in such a magnificent way. It was as though the Holy Spirit transported me to the stage. His Presence lit up the stage; lit up my soul too. My little girl issues of emotional abandonment, neglect and abuse were being washed away, as I took hold of the feet of the children. Both our fragile souls were being made clean and whole by His amazing grace and compassion, by the Father of us all. His love moves mountains and will leave heaven for the sake of the children. How Radical is that! I am grateful. But I was mentally exhausted and emotionally spent. I was in need of a touch from my Savior. By now, the nation was in an uproar over the election of, Barack Obama, the first African American president of the United States of America. It was his words of encouragement to citizens to go or return to school that got me going.

In 2009, at age sixty-two, I was encouraged to step into the steady current and culture of intentional servant leadership of Bakke Graduate University Master of Arts in Global Urban Leadership (MAGUL) graduate program. Through the pastoral wisdom and counsel of Dr. Lowell Bakke, he indicated that the Bakke culture and coursework would help settle my soul down and give me a new lens by which to serve God, family, and community. Lowell's words really did create a place of peace within the soul of this unsettled and fretful sixty-two-year-old community activist. Later in 2015, it would be the insightful healing and transforming words of Dr. Cornel West, who stated, "It took love to move the movement." Yet throughout

the early years of the civil rights movement, lynching continued throughout the south and assassinations of prominent leaders escalated. Pres. John F. Kennedy and later his brother Robert F. Kennedy and Martin Luther King Jr. and Malcolm X created heated tension and deep resentment between the races. As a child, I felt unprotected and so unsure of my future. As an older adult, I am very sure of this very thing: "The earth is the Lord's and all who dwell in it" (Ps 27:1).

In the spirit of Dr. DeGruy's comprehensive research on post-traumatic slave syndrome, I can't help but consider the damage American slavery and racism play on the psyche of all American citizens, African Americans in particular. It takes a mighty love to learn to live out one's purpose in chains, oppression, and downright brutality. How did Christ move through society of His time? He was falsely accused, smitten, beaten, scourged, and then (lynched) crucified. Yet as he hung from the cross, He spoke. "Father, forgive them, for they know not what they do." What a radical kind of love! As I enjoy the promise age of seventy, I embrace Psalm 37:25, which speaks directly and pointedly to the ordered steps of my life in Jesus Christ: "Our steps are made firm by the Lord, when he delights in our way… I have been young, and now am old, yet I have not seen the righteous forsaken or their children begging bread."

Why is this book relevant to my personal transformation? Community transformation? Radical servant leadership? This book is intended to show the intergenerational delight the Lord takes in our efforts to bring about changes that heal. It is hoped that this book will inspire older adults to move from a mindset of isolation to one of invigoration in service to God and to believe that one's latter days can truly become one's better days. This book is intended to serve and inspire the urban leader, pastor, and ministry to tap into the untapped wisdom of older adults (like Naomi and Ruth) as a viable resource for the sake of children. When I reflect on the transforming power of servant leaders, past and present, I am encouraged by God's delight in the life and work of Jesus Christ, Mother Teresa, and Dr. Martin Luther King Jr. My heart becomes full and hopeful. Our Lord and Savior Jesus Christ's acts of humility as servant in obedience to the will of the Father were active yesterday, are active today, and remains until His return. It's the makeover power, the wondrous working power of the blood of Jesus, at labor today to change and heal the heart of humanity—from one of violence to one of peace. In particular, I do believe older adults, especially grandmothers, are one of God's secret weapons of transformation in the earth realm.

Chapter 1

My Servant's Calling

Open your mouth for the speechless... Open your
mouth...and plead the cause of the poor and needy.
—Proverbs 31:8–9
(New Spirit-Filled Life Bible)

Shaping of a Servant

Well, I definitely had a militant attitude and that of an angry Black woman too! In fact, all America was filled with rage. The 1960s ushered in some pretty earth-shattering realities for this young African American girl coming of age in the small town of Vallejo, California. I was just a preteen growing up during an era of heated, painful, and deadly social and political changes. The 1960s civil rights movement and racial hatred, including violence against me personally, got this impressionable and vulnerable mind so fretful about what would become of my life.

When I was between the ages of ten and fourteen, the movement brought racial injustice and all its animosity and brutality to the forefront of my already overtaxed emotions. Marches, protests, sit-ins, beatings, lynchings, and senseless killings were repeatedly happening throughout the south, including other parts of the nation where there was a presence of African American families; and it was being televised. Violent dogs were mauling African Americans, and high-intensity water hoses were sending men, women, and children rocking and reeling and crashing against buildings and sidewalks. America was a hot mess, and soon I would be too.

During these televised moments of turbulent challenges and demands, my family huddled around the small black-and-white television set. We would sit on the cold concrete floor of the three-bedroom wartime/defense housing projects. We watched and gasped as hateful and brutal Anglo police officers use the most inhumane crowd-control methods of the time. Many African Americans were pushed, beaten, and trampled by police and were beaten with their billy clubs. As though that wasn't enough, we sat trembling as we watched men, women, and children get thrust against walls and buildings by the burning force of high-powered water hoses. In other instances, there was tear-gassing of men and women in other marches that followed. I didn't know it at the time, but these events began fueling my anger tank. A militant mindset was forming and taking shape in the deep recesses of my mind. For my sisters and me, these events were most horrifying and terror driven. We had no idea at the time we were living in such a volatile culture.

These dark events were impacting my fragile soul like grenades being thrown in a war zone. Watching these events without filters or explanations caused me to become very sad and not so hopeful of my future. Yet in an interesting way, I was encouraged by the tenacity of these African American men and women who kept rising to the call to change unjust American systems. Watching them press forward to bring change to the racial inequalities and inequities of the time was well beyond my social and spiritual capital to grasp what it meant to be so courageous.

As the people of Birmingham walked and sang, I began singing too. Through my tears, I sang, "We Shall Overcome." Over the next few years, the voices of Aretha Franklin, the Staple Singers, and others began to fill the airways with calming and reflective social justice lyrics for all America to consider—songs like "War" and Curtis Mayfield singing, "People Get Ready" along with Sam Cooke singing, "A Change Is Gonna Come." These songs and other social-justice songs helped to point my fast-beating heart in a forward moving direction. These songs served to inform and guide my distressed soul through this new and challenging landscape of social justice and racial prejudice.

University of California Berkeley was just twenty miles south of Vallejo. Student revolts and protests were common in the college town of Berkeley. College campuses across the nation challenged American government leadership to end the war and get out of Vietnam. Students were demanding that America make some humane changes to its sociopolitical infrastructure so that life would be better for all people. The emergence of the militant Black Panther Party confronted African Americans to take up arms to self-protect.

As I got a little older, I watched and listened in on numerous rallies and protests in the Berkeley and Bay Area. The messages of change were hostile and life-threatening. I kept my distance but raised my fist in solidarity to the messages of justice and righteousness. These events were creating some pretty acute and distressing social and emotional challenges for this young girl. However, I was drawn to the messages of change and equality as spoken by many, like Pres. John F. Kennedy and Dr. Martin Luther King Jr., and even to the courage of Angela Davis. I was uncertain about my future, but I kept showing up where voices demanding change, equality, and freedom were loud yet confusing.

The rough 1960s brought some revolutionary outspoken people and events onto my personal radar screen. People and places at the highest levels of government and at the grassroots level were clashing and name-calling all over the airwaves. Names like Stokely Carmichael, H. Rap Brown, Huey Newton, Bobby Seale, and Eldridge Cleaver were speaking from a place of boldness and militancy. National leaders, like CIA Dir. J. Edgar Hoover and Gov. George Wallace, and members of the Ku Klux Klan (KKK) were pouring out Racial hatred against these militant voices of the 1960s. At times, I wanted to run away, but where could I go? There was no peace at home and in the city.

In 1961, Pres. John F. Kennedy spoke these words: "Ask not what your country can do for you, but what you can do for your country." I was just twelve when these words found fertile soil in the deep recesses of my soul. That statement planted a seed of service that would continue to branch out in many and varied ways throughout my personal growth and development. Thus, when President John F. Kennedy was assassinated in 1963, I was emotionally devastated. I thought those words died within me. My unspoken anger deepened. Violence in America was sending me into a state of pessimism and anger was silencing my voice.

> I wish I could say that racism and prejudice were only distant memories. We must dissent from the indifference. We must dissent from the apathy. We must dissent from the fear, the hatred and the mistrust… We must dissent because America can do better, because America has no choice but to do better. (Thurgood Marshall)

At the young and bold age of twenty-five, Dr. Martin Luther King Jr. became God's servant who called America to face its fears and begin to make some compassionate and just changes in its treatment of poor people. He was the face and voice of the movement. I often wonder what it was like for him. He was young but prepared and informed for the call to go.

In 1963, Dr. Martin Luther King Jr. and the March on Washington for Jobs and Freedom were huge social awakening turning point in my life. My soul roused to the issues of freedom, racial equality, and access to our God-given right to the pursuit of happiness. Yet the ugly reality of racial prejudice was completely out of control. Just a month after the march, a bomb was thrown and exploded at 16th Street Baptist Church in Birmingham, Alabama, taking the lives of four little African American girls. I was shaken at my core. They were innocent, unsuspecting little girls. Evil and wickedness shows up in the most unsuspecting ways and places. Racial violence against African Americans was sending shockwaves of fear and insecurity throughout my already fretful soul. Angry because violent events that took the life of unsuspecting little girls like this one were becoming common place. Angry because at age ten through twelve I was feeling unprotected and uninformed of ways to navigate racially charged and hostile social systems in my small-town context.

Those little girls began their day with hopeful expectations of a joyful time at their local church. My soul ache at the loss of life of the precious souls of these little ones at the hands of heartless and mentally deranged white men. Racial hatred and violence are a menace to society. Save us all Lord.

Dark Side of Service

It would be five years later after the assassination of Pres. John F. Kennedy that Dr. Martin Luther King Jr. and Robert Kennedy would be assassinated too. What dreadfulness. What was the root of such hatred and disregard for human life? At the time, I was under the impression that White people had a distorted sense about race toward Black people. But after these events, it was no longer about race. Something sinister was at work toward humanity. And it concerned me deeply. Where did such anger and unforgiveness emerge? What was all the anger, brutality, and hatred all about? It would take years for me to get an understanding of the fallen nature of man, particularly as it relates to the sin of American slavery.

Yet in the midst of social justice, insecurities, and personal safety issues, my family continued their daily routines. Life in small town Vallejo, California, continued in its ebb and flow of African Americans rising early to show up for domestic work in rich Marin County neighborhoods. In addition, my mother's entrepreneurial spirit sought out and accepted odd jobs from local business and community leaders to supplement household income. She put my sisters and me to work very early to assist in ironing, babysitting, and running errands for neighbors. My father and other men showed up for their labor jobs at Mare Island naval installation base. In particular, my father maintained two janitorial jobs: one at the local *Vallejo Times-Herald* newspaper company and the other at the Greyhound Bus Station.

However, amid all the sociopolitical drama, an even more unforgiving reality was at hand. Girls coming of age in Vallejo during these tumultuous times were quite vulnerable to risky and violent assaults. My parents were working tirelessly night and day. My siblings and I were left unsupervised quite often. My parents worked from sunup to sundown and late into the night. They were so weary from domestic and janitorial work assignments they could barely supervise their household.

I don't recall any adult helping me to grasp the scope and range of the social-justice movement and protests of the time nor was my father emotionally present or aware of his daughters' vulnerability to sexual and physical violence. Where was my help? Where was my protector? I was making poor decisions based on the traumatic experiences and the unspoken anger and unforgiveness that followed.

It was during babysitting assignments where darkness reared its ugly head. I was raped by male friends of my elder siblings! On one occasion, I had phoned my mother to inform her that my babysitting assignment was over, and I was on my way home just three blocks away. It was about midnight and was very dark. As I was running fearfully across the street, a familiar car pulled up. The voice was familiar too. He asked if I wanted a ride home. Because my family knew him, I said yes without hesitation and got into the car, only to be taken to a secluded spot and raped. The rapist returned me to my home. My countenance was low. I blamed myself for not knowing better. You see, in my family and community culture, a child was expected to know right from wrong. My perceptions were obviously off. As I entered my home, my mother's voice acknowledged me, "Loretta, is that you?" She never asked me why I was so late or if I was all right. More anger was brewing and stewing up deep inside me.

Would violence like this befall even when doing good deeds? After a while, I began to question whether I was marked for a lifetime of personal devastations. More sexual violence would show up. On another babysitting assignment, I was raped again! Not once did my parents seek to learn of my sadness and growing anger and outbursts at home and at school. So in high school, I joined the Pep Club as a way to shout out my anger in some constructive way. And yet my parents pressed that service (work) to God and community were the main things. During much of my transition through adolescence, I felt invisible, devalued, and powerless.

My Early Christian Formation

It was my Sunday-school teacher, Mrs. Katie Gary, who helped anchor my soul in Christ during these times of trauma and uncertainty. I began serving in the church when I was just about five years of age. Once I could read and remember lyrics to hymns and gospels, Mrs. Katie placed me in the children's choir. Mrs. Katie ensured that my sister Johnnie and I participated in every auxiliary program and activity of the church. Each year, I was given speaking parts in seasonal events, like the Christmas pageant and Easter Sunday. In addition, my sister and I were mentored and guided on a servant's track as junior ushers and other service groups in our local church. In addition, Mrs. Katie would take my sister and me to youth-specific church conferences and outings in different cities. I became carsick on many of these road trips.

At about the age of twelve, I took the important walk down the aisle of Taylor Chapel Christian Methodist Episcopal Church and accepted Christ as my Savior. It was the practice of the local church to encourage young people coming of age to make a decision for Christ at this age. After all, church leaders would remind us that Jesus assumed his role and calling at the age of twelve. My church experiences gave me time out from the chaotic ups and downs of family life, community schisms, and America in transition.

My decision to accept Jesus as my Savior could not have come at a more important time in my life. In 1960, a family from Smyrna, Tennessee, had just moved to Vallejo, California. The parents were professionally trained in the health industry. The father was a physical therapist (first African American therapist in Vallejo), and the mother was a vocational nurse. The McDonald's had two daughters; one was my age. We became friends right away and spent a lot of time together. The following year, my parents permitted me to spend the summer in Smyrna, Tennessee, with the McDonald's. Because my father worked for Greyhound Bus Company, we were afforded the opportunity to travel by bus pass. We were too young and unaware to realize it at the time, but Jim Crow laws were in full effect as we traveled south from Oakland, California, to Tennessee.

Who Is Jim Crow?

> After the American Civil War (1861–1865), most southern states and, later, border states, passed laws that denied blacks basic human rights. It is not clear how, but the minstrel character's name "Jim Crow" became a kind of shorthand for the laws, customs and etiquette that segregated and demeaned African Americans primarily from the 1870s to the 1960s. (history.com, January 2020)

Never had I enjoyed more delights than that of a southern summer fun adventure in Smyrna, Tennessee. I was fascinated by the lightning bugs, running barefoot in the unexpected summer storms and enjoying the seeming freedom of southern summer. However, my fun was abruptly shortened by a summons from Mrs. McDonald, the mother of my new friend, Deborah. She informed me that my mother had made arrangements for me to travel by bus (alone) to Chicago to visit her mother, my grandmother, Gertrude Banks (Ms. Lucy).

After, I was taken to the bus station in Nashville, Tennessee. I experienced the terror that Jim Crow evokes on African American people. I encountered the face and presence of evil as I stood and waited to board the bus. At my age (twelve), and alone, the encounter was most frightening. A seedy-looking Anglo man slithered alongside the pillar where I was standing. He said, "Where are you going, little girl?" The moment seized my emotions. Every fiber in my body was heightened to a degree of fear that I had never experienced before. I felt vulnerable and afraid. My body froze. I couldn't move. It seemed like I stopped breathing for a moment. Accepting Jesus Christ at an early age gave me a person and power to grasp in times of troubles. At least that is the way my family and community expressed their familiarity with the man Jesus who we all called upon daily. In this instance, I didn't have my father, mother or siblings near so I called upon the name of Jesus to save me. However, the words never left my mouth. In my head and soul I was screaming for help. Jesus did save me. In the next moment the announcer over the loudspeaker broke through my immobility. It was time to board the bus. What became of this ill intention individual? I do not know. Without total recall, only God knows how I got from the pillar to a seat in the back of the Jim Crow bus.

Jim Crow laws directed me to sit in the back of the bus, and it was very crowded and tight. Needless to say, I did not sleep until we arrived at Grand Central Station in Chicago the next day. An African American mother and child sat next to me. Both mother and child slept during the entire bus trip. At times, her head would fall on my shoulder. Although Chicago was just under 470 miles from Nashville, we didn't arrive until the next day. I suppose that was a local bus. After unloading from the bus in Chicago, I found myself standing in the middle of Grand Central Station. It was so overwhelming. I was never so happy than to look up and see my four-feet-ten grandmother and her preacher husband quickly descend down the escalator to comfort and embrace me.

Chicago was alive and vibrant, hot and muggy too. My grand-mother introduced me to a nation of relatives. From one house to another, I would meet clans of cousins, mostly boys. I would sit out on the stoop of the brownstone building, talking late into the evening with one cousin who lived in the same building as my grand-mother. My grandmother would call for me. Once, I said, "I will come in when all the cars are all off the streets."

She replied, "That will be all night. So get on in here."

I chuckled and turned in obedience and followed her into the brownstone apartment building. I don't recall boarding a Greyhound bus in Chicago to return back to Nashville, Tennessee. But the Lord protected me. So I was back in the hands of the McDonald family for the long return ride to California.

My visit with my maternal grandmother was filled with intro-ductions to a seemingly never ending host and lineup of cousins and relatives in South side Chicago. Over the next five or so days of my visit, I learned and observed that my family tree was filled with lots of male relatives. Unlike my siblings, my mother had eight girls, and lastly two boys. Many of my Chicago relatives lived in public hous-ing. So did my family in Vallejo, Ca.

My grandmother was just inches over four feet tall. She was often referred to as Ms. Lucy, Bid Momma, and/or Ms. Gertrude. My grandmother was steeped in church life as a servant and inter-cessor. Her second marriage was to an alcoholic pastor-husband. My grandmother found ways to avoid his grasp when he was inebriated. Thank God she was a prayer warrior.

Adjusting to Motherhood

Four years later, I would find myself adjusting to my new role as young mother of a beautiful young African American boy. My son's father, Frank Earl, and I were dating in high school. He was a pretty popular guy. Which meant there were other girls too. Young and unaware, we plunged into the "free love" movement during the 1960s. Much later during my Christian growth and development I would learn that sex outside of marriage is a sin. Yet, God gave me, a young, seventeen-year-old single mother, strength to bear a beautiful African American son. Frank had an easy temperament. He was charming and kind. He was welcome in many of the new and different cultural circles that were showing up on my personal radar. The social-justice movement was beckoning my soul to respond. When I would take off to attend a gathering or meeting in nearby towns like Berkeley, Oakland, and San Francisco, his paternal grandparents were all too willing to care for him. They kept a nursery just for him during times when I was working in San Francisco, California. Quite frankly, my son enjoyed the quiet stability that his paternal grandparents provided. Conversely, my life was being challenged by the demand of much rhetoric and propaganda of many voices of change. My friends and I would show up on the edges of the various student-protest venues in and around Vallejo, California.

Reflections

This book-writing endeavor provides me with an expressive platform to own and tell my story of violence and redemption. Looking back on my life and the events of the 1960s, I can see how the Lord used each one of my challenging life experiences to redeem my soul and help fulfill my servant's calling and heart of compassion for the sake of children.

What I find so interesting is that in the face and presence of incredible evil and potential confrontation and even death, African Americans continued to travel to and from various parts of the nation, including travel in and out of the United States. After reading *The Collected Autobiographies of Maya Angelou*[3] with her life stories of early childhood separation from her birth mother, racial confrontations in Alabama, sexual violation, and more, I can't help but give praise to God for His redemptive grace and sustaining love over her life and over mine. As a young woman, Ms. Angelou was seemingly pressed by God to keep dancing and writing. These skills and talents connected her life to people and places like Ghana, West Africa, and Germany and other countries and continents. In doing so, she discovered an amazingly gifted phenomenal woman. Her footprint in the earth has lighted a path for little girls, African American girls in particular (including me), to keep reading and writing the stories of failure and triumph housed deep within one's soul.

At the writing of this book, the airwaves are fraught with exposure of allegations of sexual sins of our American political leaders against women and girls working in their confidence. Secret sins have a way of making it to the light. This is quite interesting as I write and tell my story of sexual sins compounded on me during my formative years.

The first twelve years of my life were shaped and influenced by God's servants who responded to the call to use their voices to speak up for the poor and oppressed during the turbulent 1960s. Three competing themes were demanding my attention and at times taking my breath: my Christian formation (trust Jesus) and the civil rights movement (take action) as well as the militant messages of antigovernment protests (take up arms).

My soul remembers the hopeful messages of Jesus Christ (the Lord is my shepherd) that were deposited in my spirit as a child and the profound messages of Mother Teresa that suggest that believers should live simply so that others may simply live, as well as the long chains of messages and sermons of Dr. Martin Luther King Jr., who expressed the dream that one day, we shall have a just society.

The one steady rock of stability was seen in the person of Mrs. Katie Gary, my Sunday-school teacher. She was always present when we would arrive at the church house. She just showed up whenever the doors of the church needed to be open and whenever the building needed heat or air. To my young mind, she never slept or slumbered. She was always there. Even when I became a teen mother at age seventeen, my local church did not reject my son and me.

It would be fifty years later that I would learn it was El Roi, "the God who sees me," who never took His eyes off me. My God kept my mental and emotional health from cracking under the chaotic and turbulent times in my home and in the nation. The God who saw me at twelve—terrified, and alone—at the bus station in Nashville, Tennessee, sees me today at seventy, encouraged and hopeful. It was El Roi then and remains He who keeps His eye on me as I move in and out of violent scenarios seen and unseen.

As He was with Hagar in the desert, so He is with me. Hagar encountered El Roi during a chaotic time of her life. She was fleeing from the presence of Sarai. Alone with her son, Ishmael, Hagar encountered the angel of the Lord. It was there that Hagar called the name of the Lord who spoke to her. "You are the God who Sees; for she said, Have I also here seen Him who sees me?" (Gn 16:13 Holy Spirit-Filled Living Bible).

I am grateful to God to share my story of redemption, renewal, and restoration—a story of encouragement to every older adult who asks and wonders if her (older) life matters to God and humanity.

Chapter 2

Creation Out of Chaos

Jesus's Calling

The creation story supports the notion that creation (creativity) emerges out of chaos (crisis). Chapter 1 of the book of Genesis captures this reality. "In the beginning God created the heavens and the earth. The earth was without form and an empty waste, and darkness was upon the face of the very deep" (Gn 1:1–2 AMP). It has been said by street prophets that perhaps God created the chaos. Perhaps something was there before our creative lives began. Nevertheless, God brings order out of chaos and darkness. After He livens up the physical universe and establishes order and harmony, He creates humanity. "Then the Lord God formed man of dust from the ground, and breathed into his nostrils the breath of life; and man became a living being." (Gn. 2:7 NASB) How radical is that? I believe God was calling me to bring order to my inner life and to the lives of young people who, through no fault of their own, were emotional mess too. In the midst thereof, my local-church politics were creating a new kind of chaos for me to contend with. New leadership in the pulpit began dismantling the five choirs Mama Smith directed.

God creates order out of chaos. It was customary for me to turn the television on high volume while in the kitchen or another room. The evening news was providing highlights of stories that would follow the commercial break. The announcer indicated that a story was forthcoming of an eighteen-month-old baby who was undergoing emergency surgery to restore a ruptured anus. I could not wrap my mind around that reality. How was it even a consideration for an adult to take advantage of a small fragile soul? I lost it! What mind could bring about such a horrible injury to such a little one? Yet deep down within my soul, I was acquainted with violence against unprotected, unsupervised, and vulnerable children.

Within minutes, the facts were revealed. Every fiber in my being went into high alert. I waited for the details of the story. As I sat before the television and listened to the details, my heart was weeping for this precious baby. What came next horrified me. The childcare worker's boyfriend was a suspect and was taken into custody. My heart broke into many pieces. I fell to the floor, sobbing and crying out to the Lord for an answer. Where were the responsible adults? I shouted to God, "How could you let such a vile act of violence come against such a fragile and defenseless baby!" Anger and sorrow flooded my soul. Why did this story move so deeply within me? I suspect it touched on old and unspoken memories of my early childhood violations. Later I will say more about the physical and sexual violence that came against me as I was coming of age during the early 1960s.

Jesus was calling. What was He asking of me? What demand was He placing on my character? What good could come forth from this grave situation? Jesus shares a parable of the lost sheep. "What man of you, if he has a hundred sheep and should lose one does not leave the ninety-nine in the wilderness and go after the one that is lost until he finds it?" (Lk 15:4–6). Yet in the heat of so much heartache and pain, Jesus called me to open my heart and home to one foster child. Although I said yes to the call to open my home and heart to one, I did so with much trepidation and fear. You see, at fifty, I was in as much need of a touch from the Father as did those precious babies.

An Ode to Mama Smith

It is the policy of the African Methodist Episcopal Church General Conference to move senior pastors every four years or so. New leadership at First AME Church brought disruptive change and the undoing of the five choirs Mama Smith directed. Mama Smith was a devout AME and had a feisty character with a passion to share her love for God with young people through music. She was a graduate of Howard University with a degree in music. She taught her choirs the mechanics and techniques of singing from your belly and dropping the jaws to get the fullness of the desired sound. Sometimes a hymnal would come flying at your head if you missed the musical mark. She taught her choirs the history and pride of the founder, Richard Allen, and influencers like Biddy Mason of First AME in Los Angeles, California. She was a volunteer docent at Los Angeles City Hall and was a social-justice activist. She was a high-energy, high-performing older adult with a passion to serve God as his radical servant leader.

Her choir members and community at large affectionately called her Mama Smith. A year after I arrived in Los Angeles, she and I met at a local community event for inner-city youth. My son and I gladly accepted her invitation to not only join her choirs but also accept her as godmother too. We needed an extended family. Two years later, at the age of ten, my son and his close friend took the walk down the long aisle of First African Methodist Episcopal (FAME) church and accepted Jesus Christ as Savior and Lord. What a joyful and happy time for me. For the next seven years, we lifted up our voices in joyful and loud praises.

The Breakup

Then came the breakup. The new pastor wanted a different sound and rhythm. There were meetings with lots of disagreements. Finally, Mama Smith surrendered to the change and stepped down as choir director. Many of her choir members left the church, including my son and I.

After sulking for nearly six months without a church home, I found a note in my mail from someone who was inviting me and my companion to a Bible study. In 1983, I began attending Bible study taught by a former militant-minded university professor and his seemingly quiet, soft-spoken wife yet radical servant leader Sherrill. She was a choir director, musician, and more. She established Family Forum, a system of care, communication, and education that equipped and strengthened congregant families during times of transitions. Today, she is licensed to serve as Dr. Mac. We remain good friends. I will say more about Sherrill and her transforming gifts and talents later. After learning the art and science of hermeneutics, how to study Scripture, along with the fallen nature of man, I quickly made some changes in the way I was casually living my life before my son. As the Word of God moved on my heart, I began to take authority over my behavior and, thus, asked my male companion to move out of the home we shared. A burden was lifted.

What I wish to express in this chapter is that in the midst of great personal loss and devastations, believers can be assured that the spirit of the living God is at work within bringing forth divine order, peace, passion, and personal transformation as well as perfecting of one's purpose in advancing the kingdom of God. The Holy Spirit midwifes our pain to bring forth a radical form of service to God, family, and community in some unique ways. Such was the proving of my faith in Christ and passion to intentionally advocate for vulnerable children.

Speak, Lord, Your Servant Is Listening

The love of God flooded my soul and began speaking to my heart for me to let Him into my stony heart so He could heal it in a most distinct way. I would learn that this horrific event would mark a major turning point in my trust and reliance on the redemptive work of Christ. A scripture that fuels my servant-leader calling is found in the book of John 21:17: "If you love Me, feed My sheep." It is motivation for me to get going with the things that matter to God.

Children matter to the Lord. Psalm 127:3 captures God's heart for children: "Children are a reward of the womb..." My heart was quickened to obedience. I committed my ways and my heart to the Lord by yielding to the call to serve vulnerable children in some direct way. The Lord was creating a story of His goodness and mercy. Something good was coming from this chaotic and horrific event. The Lord began placing me in opportunities to be in undeviating and calculated service to children.

A Social Justice Response

After sobbing so deeply for this baby, I had no more tears. Pulling myself up from the floor, I regained my composure. While listening and sitting still in my bedroom for quite some time, I let the event and God's calling marinate in my mind, heart, and spirit. Something new and different was taking shape. At age fifty, here I was being Holy-Spirit led to yield my will to a mighty assignment to pay attention and be present in the lives of vulnerable, broken, and damaged girls.

The next morning, I called a friend who had been fostering for quite a few years. I shared the previous evening's news about the baby. She had a servant's heart toward hurting children and families, so she encouraged me to step into Los Angeles County child welfare system by opening my home as a licensed foster family. She walked me through every step of connecting with the various and multidisciplinary agencies that are charged with protecting our kids. Within six months (1998), I was trained and oriented to the guidelines of hosting abused and neglected children in my home.

State of California

Department of Social Services

Facility Number: 198201455

Effective Date: 01/15/1998   Total Capacity: 1

In accordance with applicable provisions of the Health and Safety Code of California, and its rules and regulations; the Department of Social Services hereby issues

this License to

RANDLE, LORETTA

to operate and maintain a

FOSTER FAMILY HOME

Name of Facility

RANDLE FOSTER FAMILY HOME
2017 WEST 83RD STREET
LOS ANGELES, CA 90047

This License is not transferable and is granted solely upon the following:

LICENSEE MAY PROVIDE CARE AND SUPERVISION FOR ONE (1) CHILD, AGE 2-17 YEARS OF AGE; AMBULATORY ONLY. THERE IS NO POOL OR BODIES OF WATER ON THE PREMISES.

Client Groups Served:

CHILDREN / INFANT

Complaints regarding services provided in this facility should be directed to:

CCLD Regional Office   (310) 568-1807

Pamela Dickfoss
Deputy Director,   Authorized Representative of Licensing Agency
Community Care Licensing Division

LIC203A (03/07) FAS   POST IN A PROMINENT PLACE   CU-TAO18b
Print Date 08/22/2017

My home was up to health and safety codes and certified to receive infants and children. Although I received many calls to host teens, my heart and call was to be the first place of contact for infants and toddlers. I only accepted one toddler in my home. Today I still maintain my foster family license as a bridge and voice of advocacy into the complex network of the child welfare system.

Life's challenging issues abound toward and on young unsuspecting girls and single mothers living in urban cities. Violence against girls, in particular, shows up in the form of rape, child sex trafficking, violent lyrics against women, drug abuse, gun violence, and teen suicides, including school-based bullying, cyberbullying, and lots of anger outburst in public spaces. These are just a few examples of the many social-ills believers and social justice advocates must contend with when serving in urban cities around the globe.

An Urban Crisis

Many children living in urban places are angry, sad, and afraid. In one of my volunteer community advocacy roles, I often encounter young children with disruptive behaviors and expressive anger issues in my volunteer foster grandparent role at a local child development center in urban Los Angeles. A young girl of just four years old was having a most fitful anger outburst in the classroom. The teachers were unable to calm her down. The executive director was called to assist. She asked me to join her. The child was given space and time to scream, pace, and knock a few things over. The child was then placed on a seat and was consoled by both the director and me. The director has received extensive training in helping young children regain their composure after anger outbursts. In this instance, my help and assistance came as a constant gentle hand rub and an intentional whisper in her ear that Jesus loves her. Even though she knocked my glasses off my face, I maintained hand contact and continued to whisper the love of Jesus Christ in her ear. I believe in the restorative power and presence that are manifested in the spoken name of Jesus. Saying the name of Jesus has redemptive and restorative power. We walked the child to the main office. I sat with her while the office staff phoned the grandmother to come for the child. By now, the child was quiet. As we waited for her grandmother, I continued to rub her hand and affirm that her life matters to God. Once the grandmother arrived, I was off to another task. The child and grandmother were waiting in the courtyard. The child spotted me and left her grandmother and ran to me and wrapped her little arms around my legs. Nothing was spoken. Nothing was said. She and I embraced for what seemed like a very long minute, just a big hug of what felt like gratitude. My soul was touched. How radical is that!

It was the transforming coursework of my graduate-degree work in Bakke Graduate University's Master of Arts in Global Urban Leadership (MAGUL) program where the best practices of the eight core values/perspectives enlivened my soul. Incarnational leadership and servant leadership perspectives landed in an authentic way and place within me. If Christ could leave heaven, incarnate Himself by showing up in my neighborhood, seek me out, and spend time whispering His love and affection in my thirsty soul, then surely, I could do the same by whispering the love of Christ into the souls of these precious preschoolers. How radical is that! It is a lovely experience to see the children light up, fill up, then look up, and begin to share their stories. I believe in listening to children. They have stories that need to be told and heard.

Incarnational Leadership in the Midst of Chaos

In my volunteer role at Faith Children's Child Development Center in South Los Angeles, a four-year-old boy began acting out in the classroom. He was brought to the office. The director asked me to spend some time with him. We found a quiet room. After a while of listening, I took hold of his hand and asked who he was so angry with. He immediately responded by saying he was angry with his mother's friend. The night before, the boyfriend had disciplined the young boy very harshly. He expressed his displeasure and anger toward this man who was not his father. After a little while, the young boy was given a craft to further help him release and process some of his unexpressed frustrations. The practice of incarnational leadership that allows me to be present with young children is both an affirming and transforming way of connecting with them.

DreamCatcher Residential Home for Girls

They are a Native American tradition and have been around for generations. Traditional dream catchers are intended to protect people who are sleeping from negative, bad dreams while still letting the positive, good dreams come through. The good dreams go through the hole in the center of the dream catcher and then glide down the feathers to the person sleeping below. (https://winterandsparrow.com/dream-catchers/)

Young girls living in residential care facilities are angry, fearful, and headstrong, as well as prone to incredible loud and vulgar outbursts. If the Native American dream-catcher scenario is true in practice, then many of our girls living in out-of-home care are experiencing negative and fearful dreams. These fretful nights were getting the best of their mental health.

During my graduate studies in the Master of Arts in Global Urban Leadership program, I submitted an application to serve as a volunteer childcare worker at Dreamcatcher, a level 12 residential group home for girls in the foster care system. Level 12 is a designation for girls in foster care placement who require medication to settle and calm their fast-beating hearts and agitated souls. In 2011, the Dreamcatcher Foundation served as a living lab for me to test and apply the incarnational practice of being present in the lives of the least and last among us—weak and hurting girls. I received concrete understanding and sound doctrine on what it means to be a servant leader in this hard urban setting. This labeling meant girls received psychotropic drugs and heavy wrap around therapeutic services. This particular group home had three homes where girls were placed for short- and long-term periods. Emotional eruptions were common, along with girls taking off as runaways. A phenomenon was on the horizon: young people were aging out in the foster care system, and many of these young people became homeless, incarcerated, and subject to human sex trafficking.

Although I was hired as a part-time childcare worker, the executive director permitted me to define my role differently. I was allowed to introduce wellness practices, such as a relaxing cup of tea, soothing music, deep breathing, and prayer time, and for some, I was allowed to take a girl on a neighborhood walk. The executive director supported the wellness initiative by purchasing Armstrong tea kettles for each of the three homes. Three nights a week, I would show up at a designated home. Group homes experienced high incidences of runaways. After we integrated these wellness practices, the executive director of the group home confirmed with me that she noticed a decrease in the number of girls who went Away With Out Leave.

Incarnational leadership and servant leadership (SL) are pretty radical approaches of showing the love of Jesus Christ.

Embracing SL as a best practice informs and provides a practical context for me to affirm my past and present service-to-humanity life experiences. SL also informs how I move and live and have my being in urban cities on a local and global level. The gospel according to John chapter 3 states, "God so loved the world that He gave his only begotten Son…" (Jn 3:16). Moreover, Jesus speaks of His purpose as one who came not to be served but to serve.

Taking on a servant-leadership mindset within the group-home context proved beneficial to both the girls and I. At times, it would mean that I needed to just show up and be present. At other times, it could simply be sharing a smile or asking about an aspect of a girl's life—something as simple as one's favorite color, favorite food, favorite music artist, or favorite movie. These moments would allow a girl to make attempts at telling her story.

My signature health-and-wellness symbol is a tangible orange fruit. I would bring oranges on every occasion to share with the girls. Orange symbolizes the color of hope and healing. In general, these girls carried a lot of traumatic emotional pain from sexual and physical abuse and separation anxiety, including neglect and depression. So for me to have the privilege and honor to listen in on these girls' fears, faith, and hopes brought much healing to many of my unspoken memories of abuse also.

In one of my attempts to create the perfect writing space, I went to the local library. While there, two young ladies came in and sat at a table just across from me. I couldn't help but look up occasionally and smile at the one who had a young infant wrapped in a colorful cloth around her body. I was so moved by this act of seeming incredible security, comfort, and care for the child—a safe place. After a little while, the mother began unravelling the baby from the wrap, and out came this adorable small five-week-old baby girl. Well, what the mother did next caused me to stay alert. She laid the baby on the table (hard library table) and then became distracted by her cell phone. The baby made a move with her legs that might have caused her to roll off the table, so I jumped up from my seat and approached the mommy and asked if I could hold the baby. I sat and began chatting with both girls. As God would have it, these two girls said, "We think we know you. Did you ever work at a group home?

I said yes.

They exclaimed, "We were there in 2011."

I responded, "Yes, I was there at the same time."

Only the Holy Spirit could arrange such an encounter. I gave the mother a referral for her baby, and we exchanged numbers. I hope to stay in touch. God's radical love shows up in unsuspecting and odd ways and places.

Reflections

Living in a fallen world creates both challenges and opportunities of service in Christ. Living for Christ brings one face-to-face with the need to share the love of Jesus in unique ways. Incarnational leadership suggests that one shows up and is present when and where hurting people are—listening and affirming that their lives matter to God. A servant leader is one who decides to serve first then aspire to lead. Servant leadership in the context of the group home setting is inspiring girls to tell their stories. My servant's calling is to listen to their stories.

God is the Creator of us all. God creates order out of chaos (crises). Psalm 24:1 affirms, "The earth is the Lord's and all its fullness. The world and all who dwell therein." His love never fails. He is risen. He has made all things new, and He is coming back again for all those who believe that He is the Christ, the Son of the living God.

I now understand the book by Dr. Ray Bakke entitled *A Theology as Big as the City*. The city is the place to which all people flocked for help and assistance. Theologians would do well to expand their religious practices and beliefs beyond just evangelism. The church must come to understand that our Savior and Redeemer walks and lives among (us) the people who need Him the most, i.e., the sick, lame, lost, destitute, immigrant, child, homeless, forgotten, and so many more social injustices. Bakke's book certainly frames how the gospel of the kingdom of God must colonize the earth—with the love, forgiveness, and gift of eternal life to all people who will believe on the name of Jesus.

Chapter 3

Roots of Radical Servants

Before I formed you in the womb I knew you...
—Jeremiah 1:5
(New Spirit-Filled Life Bible)

My son, friends, and I sat, glued to the television set for eight weeks to witness and experience the unfolding of what seemed like an African tale; however, the television series was based more on facts than myth or mystery. To learn and know from whence one comes, from which one has beginnings, deepens one's connectivity to a sense of belonging to a greater community.

It was January 23, 1977. Millions of Americans, African Americans in particular, had tuned in to watch the new television miniseries *Roots*. The movie was based on a multigenerational journey and exploration of author Alex Haley's family tree that crossed more than a century of the African American experience from Africa to America.

God knew me. The origin of my deeper eternal roots can be found in the book of Jeremiah 1:5, "Before I formed you in the womb I knew you..." What a powerful and reassuring fact. I was approved and chosen by God to be who I am in this place for such a time as this.

God used the movie Roots to show me there is so much more to my life than my past and historical memory of American Slavery, and my present-day life experiences and woes.

My heritage and history began in the Garden of Eden. When God scooped up the dark, rich soil of Africa and formed and shaped humanity, he had me in His imagination. God knew my life would take many twists and turns. Some that could have easily taken my life. But his plans and purposes for my life are for his greater good and eternal gain.

Yes, the movie Roots help me to embrace a new and profound awareness of my Familia connections and ancestry to Mother Africa. He knew I would begin to raise up my bowed down head in honor of My Lord and King, my Creator and Maker. How radical is that.

> Jeremiah was already a young man, but God wanted him to know that his call went back even further than his youth. Jeremiah existed in the mind and plan of God before he ever existed in his mother's womb. God told Jeremiah this so that he could walk in God's pre-ordained plan by his own will. This information wasn't given just to interest Jeremiah or to entertain him. It was given so that he would know God's will, be encouraged by that, and therefore align his will with God's revealed will. (Enduring Word commentary. January 2, 2018)

Knowing one's family roots is critically important to one's sense of well-being and positive growth and development. Ongoing restorative justice and reconciliation is needed to heal the years of damage that American slavery has wrought on the American psyche, especially on African American men, women, and children. Yet history documents the servant's mindset of African Americans during this time.

Servant leadership is a deeply rooted calling of God to humanity. My servant's story is intensely imbedded in service. Jeremiah 1:5 affirms that I was called before conception and planted in the fertile soil of service to humanity. The task of framing and creating my family roots became all too important for this chapter. My historical and radical servant stories are being captured through aging bodies, with not-so-accurate memories of the details. The following pages release flickering lights of radical hope and love in the endearing stories of my forefather's births, marriages, deaths, and family dynamics. My sketchy family roots are recorded from the oral history telling of three family elders: cousin Lee Arthur Randle (eighty-five); Aunt Eva Lee Whitt (102); and bedridden, Alzheimer-bound Auntie Beatrice Randle-Phenix (103). A few of my siblings have added or recalled family-lineage memory nuggets too.

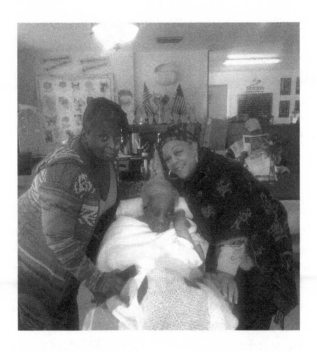

On a 2017 Thanksgiving trip to the Bay Area, I had the privilege of visiting my 103-year-old aunt, Beatrice Randle-Phenix. She lives in a nursing home in the Bay Area. She is the eldest and only living sibling of my dad, Willie Randle Jr. Although she is stricken with Alzheimer's, her son, my eighty-five-year-old cousin Lee, visits and sits with her on a daily basis. Lee is her firstborn. He may be the only living relative (that I am aware of) on my dad's side that holds sketchy family history. My cousin Lee declares that he and his mother, Beatrice, arrived in Vallejo a few years before my father and family arrived in 1947. I would grace the world the following year on August 17, 1948.

Knowing that the Lord had me in his mind, made a choice to give me life, and approved of my purpose in this world is incredibly liberating. To have this strong sense of eternal belonging and purpose for such a time as this causes me to raise up my sometimes bowed-down head. To know I am called a servant of God for such a time as this makes me want to dance. Yet in the natural sense of things, my soul wonders and yearns to know from whence does my natural family roots and origins begin. I recall driving with Prof. Wes Johnson from Seattle, Washington, to Cedar Springs, Washington. He was able to, with accurate detail, tell the story of his ancestors' immigration from Sweden to the United States and how they settled in the northern part of the United States. While I was amazed, I became a little jealous that I could not give homage to my family roots and origins as well as Professor Johnson was able to do so.

Family Origins

It was told that my father and mother and their first three young girls (Delores, Eodies, and Johnnie) arrived in Vallejo, California in the summer of 1947, a booming railway and naval shipyard town. My father was a man of few words. He had a strong work ethic. He held down two jobs seven days a week at the Greyhound Bus Station and *Vallejo-Times Herald* newspaper company. But he had a big presence as provider in our family life. Although he was rarely home or interacted with his girls, he made sure there were provisions for his family. The origins of my family roots have been seemingly fragmented by the direct and residual effects of American slavery.

It was told to me that my father's life began in Tallulah, Louisiana, on October 10, 1916. His mother, Ms. Lucy, died giving birth to her third child, Johnny Randle. Story has it that my dad and his sister Beatrice were sent to live with their paternal grandparents, Ike and Mae Lizza Randle, and Ms. Lucy's siblings (Stewarts) took care of baby Johnny. My uncle Johnny did make it out to California and lived with our family for a short while. He passed away in the 1980s. Although I never met my paternal grandfather, Willie Randle Sr., my first cousin Lee tells the story that my grandfather, Willie Randle Sr., remarried to Mary. They moved to Chicago and bore three more children—George, Clarence, and Rose Randle. My maternal great-aunt Eva Lee Whitt tells the story that my mother and father met somewhere along the Mississippi River, in or around Natchez, Mississippi. Story has it that they fell in love around the early 1940s. My eldest (deceased) sister, Delores, was born in 1943; my second eldest sister, Eodies, was born in 1945; and my third eldest sister, Johnnie Ruth, was born in 1947. I, Loretta Beatrice Randle, would be the fourth-born child and firstborn in California. Six more children would follow: Regina Matteel, twins Gwendolyn Lee and Eileen Marie, Sharon Denise, Mark Anthony, and Brian Keith. My mother, Matteel Brown-Randle, was born in the city of or on the plantation of Eutaw, Mississippi, on April 20, 1923. My mother was the eldest of three siblings, with Murdell and Robert Junior. Her mother, Gertrude Byas-Brown (Ms. Lucy), was born on October 25, 1903, in Wayside, Mississippi. My maternal great-aunt Eva Lee Whitt tells the story that her brother, Robert "Bobby" Brown (my grandfather), was born on August 1, 1901. After my grandparents married, they were challenged with the great responsibility to raise four younger siblings: Carrie, Eva, Robert, and Johnny Addison. They were raised right along with my mother and her two siblings.

At twelve, I had the privilege to meet my maternal great-grand-mother, Sophia Byas. Our meeting was in the summer of 1961 during my Greyhound bus travel from Nashville, Tennessee, to Chicago, Illinois. At the time, Mama Sophie appeared to be in her eighties. Story has it that Alfred and Sophia Byas had seven live births: Benita Ellis, Eddie Lewis, John, Gertrude, Robert, Alfred, and Samuel Byas. I met two of whom besides my grandmother Lucy (Gertrude): Uncle Alfred and Uncle Thomas. At the time of her death, Mama Sophie's age was estimated to be over one hundred. She was a feisty old girl.

Service to America

My father, Willie Randle Jr., served America in World War II as a cook in the United States Army. It is told that my father, mother, and first three siblings arrived in Vallejo, California, during the time that it was a new, booming railway and naval shipyard installation. We lived in temporary military wartime defense housing. It was called Floyd Terrace projects. Each building was of the same color inside and out. They looked like barracks. Some had two and three small bedrooms. Large families of five or more lived in these types of housing. They were nothing like the tenement building in New York or Chicago. I happen to believe that large family size was encouraged to satisfy the growing demand of the needed labor pool for domestic workers for wealthy Marin County residents, laborers at Mare Island Naval Shipyard, C&H Sugarcane Refinery, and other large industrial manufacturers.

My mother gave birth to eight girls and two boys, in that order. My mother's hands of service formed and shaped all eight of her girls' skill sets at becoming service workers, like her and my dad and like society was mandating of African Americans. My father would die of lung cancer in the summer of July 1970.

A Child Shall Lead

From age five to sixteen, I only knew God as angry and full of wrath. The messages at the time placed extreme pressure on young minds like mine to give your life to Christ so you won't go to hell. So at the appointed time, we, a group of young hellish adolescents, gave our lives to Jesus Christ. However, our behavior did not change right away. At every opportunity, one or two girls would give the index-finger sign, indicating a need to go to the bathroom, only to run two blocks to the local corner store and use our offering to make a purchase of chewing gum or hard candy.

LORETTA B. RANDLE, M.A.

Coming of Age in Vallejo

A change had come to the Randle household. Between 1960 and 1971, my parents' household was bursting at the seams. My mother's first five girls came of age quite quickly during the early 1960s. Each became teen mothers by the time we were sixteen, and our younger sister became pregnant at age fourteen. During this same season, my mother was still quite fertile. After giving birth to eight girls, she gave birth to her first son, and my first brother, mark Anthony Randle, in 1960. Then the following year, at age sixteen, my eldest sister gave birth to Gary. A year after that, my second eldest sister, Edie, gave birth to Preston. Within a year, my sister Edie was married. My mother was still fertile. In 1963, my mother gave birth to her tenth and last child and my second brother, Brian Keith. The following year, my third eldest sister, Johnnie, gave birth to Jerald, and I gave birth to my son, Frank, in 1965. In addition, and surprising to me, a week after my son was born, my sister Regina, number five, gave birth to her daughter Devon at age sixteen.

Clearly there was a social, cultural, and moral dynamic going on, not only in my family but also in my neighborhood and community at large. It was as if a rain cloud of fertility seeds poured over the wombs of young girls in my small town of Vallejo, California, in general, and the community of Floyd Terrace in particular. Nearly half of my graduating class at Vallejo Senior High School were pregnant and gave birth before, during, and/or right after high-school graduation. I do not have data to support my observation and personal experience of the number of girls who used the abortion clinics as a means of birth control. But girlfriend storytelling confirms a host of young girls who became young mothers, including our personal confessions too. Between the civil rights movement demanding expedient change in its treatment of African American people and regarding access to quality education, housing, employment, and health care, infused by the free love hippie culture of San Francisco, young girls and young boys coming of age in my community were seemingly forced into the middle of a social and cultural revolution that we did not comprehend.

I was able to cover my pregnancy through the first seven months of the school term. The two summer months off from school gave me time to wrap my head around this new phenomenon. I would soon be a mother. It was not planned or expected, nor was I being informed. Even though a social worker was sent to our home to ask if any of my sisters and I wanted to give our children up for adoption and my immediate response was no, my younger sister considered it. She was admitted in a home for unwed mothers in San Francisco, but near her time of delivery, she changed her mind. I'm so glad she did. Her daughter Devon is an incredible high school teacher in the Washington, DC, area, with three high-performing children.

To be sure I would not miss graduating on time, I enrolled my pregnant self in a summer class in 1965. Mind you, my sister above me gave birth to her first son in 1964, and my sister under me gave birth to her daughter just weeks after my delivery. So you see, my family home was bursting with children having children. And so were my close friends and classmates.

Nipsey

My son's birth in 1965 at Solano County Hospital was intense. Girls in labor were screaming bloody murder throughout the halls of the maternity ward. When the pain from the contractions would move on me, I would grab the pillow with my teeth and hold on to the side of the bed and bury my sounds into the pillow. No instructions were given. My mother's family nor the father of my son's family were present during his entrance into this world. My sister Edie did come and visit the day after. When it was time to be discharged from the hospital, my mother drove my six-pound joy and me home. On the way to our overcrowded living space, my mother made a stop at my son's paternal grandparents' home a few miles from our government housing. Elated to see her new grandson, Mrs. Johnny Watkins gazed into my son's face with a big smile. She immediately gave my son the affectionate nickname of Nipsey. Nipsey Russell was a famous Black actor and comedian during the 1960s.

My son was born on August 27, 1965, and within six weeks, I returned to school to complete my twelfth-grade academia. Six weeks was the expected term for a woman who had given birth to return to her normal duties. I enjoyed my quiet time and intimacy with my son for the few weeks. My mother instructed me to permit my eldest sister, Delores, to care for my son while I returned to school. My eldest sister had, just a few years prior, become a young mother herself of two sons. She had secured her own apartment in the same government dwellings. Many of my fellow students, Black and White, gave birth during the free-love era of the 1960s.

A Bitter Seed

Early one Saturday morning, my sister and I were awakened by a loud, quick disrupting knock at our door. Our sleep was rattled, and our fight-or-flight emotions went into high gear. We could hear our names being called and the voice saying, "Come quickly! Your father is hurting your mother." Usually, on Saturday mornings, my siblings and I could sleep a little later than our normal school-week schedule. I was just about age thirteen or so. My sister Johnnie was fourteen or so. She and I jumped to our feet and ran out the door to where the cars were parked.

My young impressionable mind was deeply impacted by an act of domestic violence at the hands of my father against my mother. What I saw next staggered me. My mother was on the ground underneath my father's car. He was kicking at her as though she was a dog. I was so fixated on this scene I could not move or speak. What had brought this behavior on with my dad? He was a man of few words and not present emotionally, but he was still my dad. Why was my mother underneath the car? Why did he want to hurt her? In the next instance, my sister Johnnie rose up to my dad and told him to stop. Just as quickly as she said it, he stopped.

In an instance of seeing this scene, I felt a bitter seed of unforgiveness and insecurity land in the ripe, vulnerable soil of my mind. This sight led me to make an interior decision that I was not safe. I could no longer trust or look to my dad as my protector. Over the years, this bitter seed would grow into a strong, angry militant mindset, which manifested in promiscuous and rebellious behavior. It would take the next fifty years before I would surrender all my hurts, fears, and damaged emotions to the Lord.

Reflections

It has been said that a father's role is to provide sustenance, protect his family from harm of predators, and seek God in prayer over and for his family. If this is so, then my father was sorely lacking in these three areas. Today, I see how important it is for a father to have a presence, a covenant role over his family, especially his girls. Otherwise, vulnerable families like mine become easy targets of prey to the human predator. I asked then, "Where was my Savior we sang to and about on Sunday mornings? Was he dead and still hanging on the cross?" Today, I can say He lives, and he lives within my heart. His reckless love pursued me, healed me, delivered me, and reconciled me as His beloved.

Chapter 4

My Radical Girlfriends

Those who pray with you in the drought
deserve to dance with you in the rain.

—Unknown

Thank God for up close and personal girlfriends. There were several friends who stood together, cried together, prayed together, and laughed together during the era of the civil rights movement during the summer of 1965 and forward, including my siblings. In addition to my siblings were my friends Linda, Deborah, Peggy, and Connie. Together we navigated our lives through the land mines of social change and personal challenges. We were vulnerable young girls coming of age. The times of social change placed our unsuspecting souls in harm's way. Many of us were wooed into believing we were loved, and engaging in sex would settle our longing to be loved and protected. Since I began writing this book, I have interviewed several friends from Vallejo and learned that many girls who came of age in the 1960s in Vallejo were raped, some violently. Some were even violated by local law enforcement officers too. The truth about social justice and change is that it comes with a price and a sacrifice.

Like the rest of the nation's youth culture, we were in search of self, personal peace, and world harmony. Marijuana use became the bridge over troubled waters. Under the influence, we pondered our future and the future of America. Would we live or die? What was the hatred all about? Why were White folks so angry and wicked? We would spend many hours (under the influence) debating, discussing, and attempting to discern the matters of the world. Together we forged closer bonds to help one another cope with becoming teen mothers, finishing school, and finding work during an era of change and uncertainties during the 1960s and onward. Sixty years later, we are still close friends.

Homage to My Siblings

But first, a word of affirmation to my siblings: Delores, Edie, Johnnie, Regina, Gwen, Eileen, Sharon, Mark Anthony, and Brian Keith. Against great odds, each one prevailed against the social-cultural limits placed before us. Living in close quarters under adverse conditions, we forged a bond of love and safety when trouble would rise in one of our lives; and trouble came often. Although Delores was a twenty-five-year survivor of breast cancer. She passed in 2004 from lung cancer. Her elder role was intense, and at times, her reputation in the community was seen as very mean and demanding. My mother placed a great deal of responsibility on her to take care of her younger siblings when my parents were away at their many and varied jobs. She was a teen mother of two sons, Gary and Daniel. One is a law enforcement official, and the other, a culinary entrepreneur and jack of all trades. My sister, Delores, did ascend to a career as a dental hygienist and later established a catering business service to small parties throughout the Bay Area.

Edie, my second eldest sibling, was quiet and seemingly timid. She was a teen mom and was married within a year to her children's father. Today she has pushed past a number of sociopolitical cultural limits. She is a retired California State Prison workers' compensation employee, and today—alongside her second husband, Joe—she enjoys the pleasures of building, growing, and cultivating five acres of land that produces fruits, vegetables, and florals. She takes pride in canning her fruit harvest as Christmas gifts to her siblings and close friends. She is a grandmother of eleven and has a servant's heart.

Johnnie Ruth, my third eldest sibling, and teen mother of three. As children, she and I enjoyed the ups and downs of early Christian-formation life at Taylor Chapel CME Church in Vallejo, California. The church was founded by a woman. My sister has incredible fortitude and inner strength. Of all my siblings, she has endured the grief of burying her twelve-year-old daughter from early childhood onset of leukemia in 1991 and the death of our mother in 1999; her husband, LJ Johnson, in 2001; and her eldest son in 2015. She currently serves in three servant roles in her local church context. In addition, she has been employed within the Social Security Administration for fifty years. We jokingly say, "They will have to carry you out before you retire." She is a radical servant too. She is generous, compassionate, and hospitable and sings like a songbird.

Regina, my fifth born sibling, and teen mother of two. As a young child, she would reside off and on with my dad's sister (I'm told it was for tax purposes). Regina is a creative soul. She loves to sing and sings very well. My mother took note of Regina's singing ability and asked the local musician at a large Baptist church in Vallejo to give her lessons. This worked out well for my sister. She continued to develop her singing talent but later decided not to pursue a singing career because of her first priority—her two children, Devon and Damon. She worked hard and long and retired with GE Supply as an internal sales engineer. In addition, she was a servant leader at Perfect Liberty, an oriental church context, for the past thirty years. Surprising to me was her pregnancy at the same time during my pregnancy. She gave birth to her first child just ten days after my son's birth. Today Regina sings at local events in the Bay Area and has developed a talent as family and friends' caterer.

My younger siblings, the twins Gwendolyn Lee (deceased) and Eileen Marie, pursued successful careers in telecommunications industry with PAC Bell and as a California Highway Patrol communications manager. My youngest sister, Sharon Denise, received a pampered education that included travels abroad. My brother, Mark Anthony (deceased), ninth sibling, lived generously. He loved baseball and had dreams of one day playing professionally. He loved baking cookies and learned the art and science of Horticulture. He has one son, Mark Anthony Randle, Jr. and several grandchildren. Later in life he married Nita Dauyon. My brother Brian Keith, tenth, and last sibling, is a self-taught musician. He is a drummer, guitarist, and sings very well. He and wife, Inga (another creative soul), formed a band and singing group. They perform regularly at venues in the Sacramento area. Brian and Inga are amazing parents of an incredible son, BJ. Brother Brian is a retired Sheriff in Sacramento, CA. Each one of my siblings use their gifts and talents to shine the love of Christ brightly in a dark world.

Linda the Culinary's Daughter

My longest and dear friend Linda tells the story that we met at about the age of five or six. She recalls her mother giving her instructions on how to get to school. Her mother worked as a trained culinary chef at the nearby military base. Linda is the second eldest of five girls. She was left alone to navigate her way to Flosden Elementary School in Vallejo. Linda was crying because she could not find her way to school. I came along and took her by the hand, and we walked to school together. I have no recall of such an event. The story is more than amazing for me to hear because I, too, was left alone to get to school by myself. At times, I was afraid of the squawking black birds who occupied the trees by which I had to travel. Our school was just three to four blocks away, but when you are so young and so small, even small steps seem too big. How I found my way to Linda, only God knows. You see, at early ages, children had to learn to rise up early and self-direct, prepare breakfast, dress, and not be late getting to school. In a household of several girls, getting to the bathroom was a big competition. It seems I did not wish to push and shove for access, so I waited, which often meant I was late for school. Our parents had already left at the break of dawn with car pools for their daily domestic work in wealthy communities like Marin County. Stories like this were commonplace in my community. Linda and I gave birth to our children just eight days apart. My younger sister Regina and Linda gave birth just a day apart. At age seventy, Linda and I look back often at our childhood, adulthood, and now elderhood; and while laughing at some of our life experiences, we exhale and give God much thanks for his keeping grace and mercy over our lives and our friendship.

Peggy, the Preacher's Daughter

Peggy's friendship began when we were in the ninth grade, around the year 1962. She tells the story that she was one of many girls who tagged along with my sister Regina and friend Deborah and me the day we decided to miss school. What started out to be a late start quickly became a large group of girls who decided to spend a day of joyriding and carousing. Peggy tells the story that she wanted so badly to be one of the "cool" girls, so she decided to ditch school that day also. Her father was a local Baptist pastor and insurance agent. I just learned about twenty years ago that Peggy was included in the "bad girls" day out too.

By the end of the school day, many of us tried to blend in with kids walking home from school, but word of our day out from school had reached our parents well before we arrived home. The entire community was lying in wait for each one of us to show our faces. Of course, my home was the place to hold court, and needless to say, we were all punished severely. My father was called. I had never witnessed this kind of anger and rage in my dad's eyes. The look in his face had terror written all over. Just that alone frightened me more than the whipping. Without looking, he grabbed the first thing his hand touched. It happened to be the rubber from around the wringer washing machine. He held me up in one hand like a chicken being ready to deep-fry. As I look back at this scenario, today my father would be jailed for the brutal beating I received. Throughout the night, my body jerked and reacted to a trauma I had never known or ever wanted to experience again. In an attempt to show some compassion for his harsh reactions, my father brought me ice cream and cookies to help me recover. My mind was made up. I did not have a father I could trust to protect me. His actions were just as violent as the enemy against whom Black folk were protesting.

Screams and wailings could be heard from many households in our neighborhood. Some girls were severely whipped with telephone cords (the old thick black ones), while others were whipped with branches from trees. As I ponder the severity of our punishments, I can't help but wonder if the rage and terror I witnessed in my father's eyes were the result of pent-up fear and anger from the injustice of racial hatred he experienced as a young man growing up in the hellish south of Mississippi and Louisiana, as well as the prejudice he surely experienced as a serviceman in the United States Army. He unloaded his unexpressed anger on my fragile four-foot-ten-inch body that crushed my soul and confidence in him as my sure protector. The violence coming against me was way over the top. When I reflect on Dr. Joy Degruy's research on post-traumatic slave syndrome, I must give consideration to the compounded and residual effects of American slavery on the psyche of my father in particular. Violence was becoming a roommate in my life and community. How much more of this could I endure? What was my story? What was my song? It was hard for me to continue singing one of my favorite hymns "Blessed Assurance." I was not giving God the glory.

Deborah the Nurse's Daughter

My friendship with Deborah began when her family relocated to Vallejo from Nashville, Tennessee, in 1960. Her parents were professionally trained as health professionals. Our families crossed lawns and visited each other's homes. Deborah's mom was multitalented too. She was a hairdresser as well as a vocational nurse. The exchange of help from Deborah's mom to help my mother with hair care was a relief and a blessing.

Deborah's family embraced me as a god sister. Deborah's family seemingly had different or quality education than my family. They spoke to one another in a way that was easy and kind, whereas members of my household yelled and screamed short staccato demanding statements. As an adolescent, I found relief in Deborah's home. It was quiet and orderly. My mother permitted me to travel with Deborah's family to and from Vallejo, California, to Nashville, Tennessee, on two occasions. Deborah was the first of our friend circle to have a baby in 1964. She was fifteen when she gave birth to her first son, Louie. His father died the following year.

The three friends mentioned above have been with me during the hard times and have celebrated with me during the high moments of my life. Each one of us is celebrating a birthday milestone of age seventy this year. We can confidently say our friendship has endured the floods and waves of change and personal challenges and the pangs of transformation.

When I suddenly and abruptly packed up my belongings and relocated to Los Angeles, California, within months my friends made their first road trip to support my move, these same friends have journeyed to my home each summer to experience our lives as friends, to create new experiences to laugh out loud, and to cry and mourn and pray together when we hurt or experience a loss of sorts. To these friends, I am grateful. They are pretty, radical servant girl-friends. There are many more friends and loved ones, I give thanks to God for holding my son and I up then, and who continue to cover us in prayer today. Friends Vallejo, and friends made in Los Angeles, and as far as Atlanta, GA, Washington, D.C., and Africa, including those who are now in heaven. I give thanks to the Creator of us all.

Reflections

Reflecting on my early beginnings and family roots, I can see God's hands were at work then as they are today, forming and shaping my servant's heart. My ancestors' and parents' radical acts of service in America, in the face of hostile and demeaning times, are commendable and show incredible resilience infused by the breath of the Holy Spirit. Like the blacksmith hammering the anvil with fire and strength, our souls were being purged and reset by the Lord.

Although societal policies and behavior of the 1960s gave way to creating shame on families like mine—children who were exposed to early sexual sins—I can't help but think about how other social determinants have played a role in helping to create some of the scenarios by which my family was confronted (like early teen pregnancy, poor nutritional access, and the trauma of racial disparities, past and present) and how these elements helped fuel some of the behaviors and choices expressed in this chapter. These same issues remain a social justice concern in the twenty-first century.

What remains encouraging to me is the presence of faith, community, and fortitude of my girlfriends and siblings to not only survive but also thrive in the face of oppression. God's grace and mercy kept us then and keeps us today, but until I could get a hold of God's recreative principle of bringing order out of chaos, shame, and a bowed-down head were the garments I wore (off and on) for nearly forty years.

In Memory of My Sister Delores

Chapter 5

Deep Calleth unto Deep

Deep calleth unto deep at the noise of thy waterspouts:
all thy waves and thy billows are gone over me.

—Psalm 42:7

Crash! Glass hitting the floor! An arm through the kitchen window! For a few seconds I was immobilized. Screaming, I ran barreling out the front door to seek help from my next-door neighbor. Only to nearly collide with the intruder. Screaming louder I turned and ran in the opposite direction. A break-in in my east Oakland apartment was happening right before my eyes. As I stood on the sidewalk of East 23rd Street I was shaking, crying and feeling helpless. I thought, *someone is trying to kill me.* Not one porch light or window shade rose up to my cry of distress. I whimpered, help me Jesus.

It was a warm summer Labor Day weekend in 1972. I was looking forward to enjoying time off from work life. A break from my weekday morning drive from Oakland to San Francisco. My seven-year-old son and I were engaged in family fun activities at my mother's home in Vallejo, CA. Whenever my siblings and our children gathered together there was always singing, shouting, boys running to and from with lots of laughter too. My son enjoyed being with his clan of 10 cousins. Then the phone ranged, and disrupted my enjoyment and peace. It was from the man I was in a very oppressive relationship with. He wanted to see me and said right away. I was to meet him at my apartment in Oakland, CA. He was demanding and manipulative. Quite frankly I had begun to feel fearful and intimidated by him. I had become agitated and disquieted on the inside. Every fiber in my body was telling me to call it quits! At the time I did not have the courage or words to speak boldly. He was abusive in many ways. Frequently he would bring his two well trained and beautiful black Dobermans over and leave them to guard me. If I moved, they growled at me. several months into the relationship I learned he was a married man, and a wanna-be pimp. After arriving at my apartment, I paced for nearly two hours. I was doing a lot of self-talk and praying for courage to let him know it was over. The circumstances under which we met were based on a fabricated lie of distress. At age twenty-three, and young mother, I was quite naïve and gullible, and angry from early childhood violence. I would later learn from my therapist and pastoral counseling that my anger, shame and unforgiveness were blinding my ability to judge character and motives of others.

During this same period of time, I was enjoying a good and steady stream of work-life employment opportunities in the thriving city of San Francisco. Thanks to the consistent social change advocates of the time, the ERA (Equal Rights Amendment) provided access to new socio-economic resources. Jobs in San Francisco were plentiful. Thanks to my parents' example, I had developed a strong work ethic and was trainable. Employment agencies were quickly established and charged with fast tracking the new labor pool of African Americans with entry level skills. In the social backdrop and airways, marches against the Vietnam War escalated during these unstable times. Nonviolent protests for freedom, equality and equity, led by Dr. Martin Luther and other leaders of the Civil Rights Movement, increased. So did police violence against marchers and protestors escalate and was regularly televised. Although these events agitated my already fretful soul, I added my angry voice to the ebb and flow of social change chants and activism. In the midst of these roaring events, a curious sense of freedom to explore the seemingly liberating paced cultural explosion had awaken in me too. My girlfriends and I were in search of meaning and purpose of our lives, for the sake of our mental health and our new responsibility as young, inexperienced parents. We listened and followed (on the periphery) the impact of the propaganda of the Black Panther movement demands for justice for African Americans in particular. At times we'd show up around Hippie gatherings in and around the Berkeley/Oakland and San Francisco area. Marijuana flowed freely. Philosophical discussions ensued about ways to pursue world peace. Promiscuity was openly rampant, too. Angela Davis's voice was resonating deep within my soul. At the time I didn't know what to do with her model of leadership. She was keenly intellectual, articulate, politically astute, and bold black woman with courage to speak her truth. I tucked it away for a later day.

The Civil Rights Movement stressed the importance of having equal rights to education. I kept an active enrollment status at local community college night courses. My employment history included four large major corporations in the financial district of San Francisco. I recall my father saying, find a job and stick with one. But my soul was so disquieted. Fear based decisions had become a common practice for me. Looking for the right fit (and potential man), I continued to move from one job to the next. My first job was with Bank of America International. My last job, before moving to Los Angeles, was with KCBS Radio station. My second job was at an insurance company where I was hired as a file clerk and worked in the basement. On my lunch hour I would go to HR and ask to practice my typing. I wanted out of the windowless basement. Several months later HR would summons me to test for an open position as a policy typist. I was promoted to the policy typing pool. My third work-life experience would be with an insurance rating bureau. The place where I would encounter, meet and become mesmerized by the fast talking, wit and storytelling abilities (lies) of the character that would soon draw me into his risky lifestyle.

At the insurance rating bureau, callers would inquire about the latest insurance rating information on a particular structure. It was my responsibility to pull the file and grant the caller with specific rating information. Well, on this particular day, I received a call with an interesting request. the caller shared a story of finding a package that appeared to be of importance. He said, it looked as though it had falling off the back of a postal truck. He emphasized the package was badly damaged. Otherwise, he would have taken it back to the post office. He asked what should he do. I knew that management had been pressing a particular agent to get his reports in on time so I extended a helping hand. In my naivety and curiosity, I asked if he would bring the package to my sister's home in Richmond where I was staying.

This little country girl became intrigued by the character's gift for gab, and seeming goodwill to be a good Samaritan. After the package was delivered, this stranger, yet energetic man, invited me out to dinner. I accepted, perhaps a little too quickly. Over dinner, I learned he was a working man as a Long Shoreman and a skilled electrician. In this instance it seemed safe enough to trust him. After a little wine, I gave into his sexual advances. My future looked hopeful. Several months later he helped me find a nice apartment duplex in east Oakland. I enrolled my son in the local elementary school. An older neighbor provided childcare for my son before and after school. My siblings and friends helped me decorate my first little apartment. For a few months my son and I enjoyed the peace and pleasure of our own place. I was hopeful.

Months into the relationship, aggressive and controlling behavior, sexual coercion and verbal abuse began to emerge. I would soon learn he had a fantasy of living a hustler's life. So began evenings out at night clubs, among other like-minded men and their women. Including road trips with couples to gambling casinos in Reno and Lake Tahoe. My life was sinking deeper into sin, and further away from God and my family. How would I get out of this toxic relationship? I believe the break-in provided a necessary confrontation for me to awaken to the voice of God calling me to make a choice. Deep calleth unto deep. The Holy Spirit reach down from on high and drew me out of the mighty roaring waters of dangerous liaisons. Standing on the sidewalk of East 23rd street, skimpily dressed in my hot pants, alone and trembling, the love of God shinned his light on my life. In that instant the Spirit met me and ask me to choose light or darkness. The future of my life was on the line. It was in the instance of a real threat of death that I heard the voice of the Lord loud and clear say, *if you don't leave now, you will surely die.* That night I chose life. I chose to return to the Lover and Protector of my soul.

A young single mother without a protector was a recipe for dangerous liaisons. I was just twenty-three or so. I would later learn I had become a negative target for way too many risky encounters with this man. Further, I was putting my son at risk too. In that instance, I declared I had had enough of him and Oakland. A quick decision was made to pack up my apartment and sever my relationship with this man who lived dangerously on the dark side.

Calls were made to the police and to two of my siblings who lived within ten to fifteen minutes of my apartment. In this terrorizing moment, I was making critical decisions about what items I would take, give away or discard. Now in the midst of all this chaos, this character had the audacity to show up at my door. He was making unsuccessful attempts at trying to force me to leave with him. Thank God for a praying mother. My sisters and their mates were present. Having family present gave me an extra boost of confidence to say no. It is over. Everything that I could not pack in my little yellow 1971 Volkswagen, I kindly gave to my sisters or left for whomever wanted it. My adrenaline was flooding my brain to get out of Oakland, and this man, and go now, in my heighten state of fight or flight mode I drove to Vallejo. It was late into the evening, and as I was crossing the Carquinez Bridge to Vallejo, I was blinded by the flood of tears wailing up in my eyes. I pulled off at the first exit. I was led to go to my girlfriend Linda's and cry on her shoulder. When she answered the door, and before collapsing. I mumbled, "someone is trying to kill." She held me up and led me to a comfortable place on her sofa for me to rest. She gave me a something that settled me down. I went into a deep sleep. When morning came, I rose up, folded the blankets, and drove farther to my mother's home. I had much to think about.

Several weeks later I received a call from Connie a good friend from Vallejo who was living in Berkeley, California. She had heard of my plight and invited me to stay at her apartment for a short while. She had been away in Los Angeles working at University of

California Los Angeles and had recently moved back to the Bay Area. I needed the time to restore and recover my mental health. She worked for UC Berkeley at the time. We spent evenings and days in deep reflection over the paths our lives had taken and what would become of us in light of the sociopolitical unrest in America, and yes, marijuana assisted and inspired us in these deep conversations. Smoking marijuana only gave me short term relief. I needed lasting peace down deep in my soul.

The character I had called it quits with had now become a stalker. He was constantly harassing me by phone calls at my workplace.

During a short season of contemplation at my friend's place in Berkeley, I decided to send my son to live with his paternal grand-parents in Vallejo. Of course, they were happy their golden grand-child was in their safe and secure arms of grace. I was glad also, even though at times, I began having feelings of not being fit to raise my own child. But again, my community of family and friends sur-rounded my woundedness like critical-care nurses.

The unspeakable happened again—another break-in. Connie's beautiful paintings and wall art were stolen. My soul was griev-ous. How do I break this pattern of devastation? Now my friend is impacted by this psycho! but thank God for the Gospel of Jesus Christ being firmly planted in my spirit as a young girl. I believe my decision to accept Jesus Christ as my Savior early in my life gave me inner strength to call on His name in these troubling times. In this instance, the Holy Spirit settled it in my heart with peace and resolve to make a big change and relocate further away.

Deep Calls to Deep

One roaring event after another was sending me into a frantic and anxious state. "Deep calleth unto deep at the noise of thy water-spouts: all thy waves and thy billows are gone over me" (Ps 42:7). Weighty waves of distress were overwhelming my mental health. What on earth was going on? Yet in the midst thereof, the spirit of Christ was moving deeper still within me—calling me, wooing me, and assuring me of His love and that He was the keeper of my soul.

Songs of deliverance flooded my soul (i.e., "Jesus Loves Me" and "What a Friend We Have in Jesus"), yet I found myself running in the opposite direction of the voice of the Lord.

Months later, while resting and recovering in Berkeley, a family friend from Vallejo rang the doorbell and asked if he could stop in and use the restroom. It was common for friends to show up unannounced. Friday nights were usually a time to play board or card games with friends. No reason to suspect any harm or foul play would ensue. But a wolf in sheep's clothing was present. My roommate was out for the evening. As I waited to usher him out the door, he made a quick turn toward me and jerked me around by my hair. I fought back with a fierceness and strength that rose up in me that was unfamiliar to me. But, strengthened I fought. This little five-footer and a six-footer were tussling on the floor. Then wicked intent was revealed. With clutches of my hair in his hand and clutches of his hair in my hands, the demon spoke: I hate you. I responded likewise, "I hate you too." He released my hair and left. Using friends of my family, I became acutely aware the demons were trying to crush my spirit. It was not working. This caterpillar girl was having difficulty changing into her butterfly, but her transformation was on the horizon. Change of place and space was calling me very loudly, and I must do it quickly. Stretched out in the middle of the floor, I began to cry out, Jesus, where are you? My roommate came in about 30 minutes later to find me in a state of shock.

My employer at the time was CBS Radio in San Francisco, California. I had confided in one of my workplace friends that I needed to leave the area. She spoke with her boss about referring me to their sister station in Los Angeles. I flew in for an interview but did not accept the offer. Another workplace friend shared her godmother's name and number with me. I decided to take a ride to Los Angeles to meet and greet my friend's godmother. It was her community-activism spirit that took hold of my desperate-for-change soul. She had two daughters and was willing to share her very large two-story home with my son and I.

By May 1973, my yellow Volkswagen was packed and was on the way to Los Angeles, California. This unknown place would soon provide me with a steady stream of emotional and spiritual redemptive experiences and harsh, transforming challenges too, including heavy demands as a social justice activist. For me, Los Angeles would become a safer place of refuge, away from those who did not know me, and a place where my personal transformation would become grounded and would flourish.

So, I thought Girls coming of age are dreaming of becoming or doing something magical, and exploring the creative, not so for me. My formative years were disrupted quite often by many life experiences brought on by family dysfunction, local and community changes, including national social/political chaos. But I was intent on recapturing, or at least experiencing the joys and wonder young girls have a right to discover. A year after getting settled into Los Angeles, one of my very first cultural enrichment activities I pursued was a weekend tap-dance class at Los Angeles City College. Although I was well into my mid-twenties, I was determined to realize and appreciate some of the joys of the creative: art, dance and more. My self-esteem needed a jump start on my new life. Although, my girl-friends supported me in this endeavor, we laughed and joked about me taking a step into this childlike fantasy of mine.

Divided against Myself

It would take years before I would surrender my oughts against others to Christ. Although I was in a new place, my behavior and choices were still out of order. I had been so traumatized by early sexual violence that I found myself making poor choices from a place of fear. Now I was divided against myself. My unresolved anger and unforgiveness against family and friends were arresting my judgment. I was concerned how my decisions were impacting my son's point of view, Yet my rebellious behavior did not change for quite some years. It would take some creative therapeutic approaches to help me discover the core of my unresolved issues were rooted in anger and unforgiveness against my parents' duty to protect me.

After about nine months of living with Margaret and her two girls, I rented an apartment in the hub of Los Angeles. We moved into a two-bedroom apartment near the intersection of Slauson and Crenshaw Blvd. in Los Angeles. I oriented my son to catching the bus to his new school: Kawaida Educational Center on Crenshaw Boulevard near Martin Luther King Boulevard in Los Angeles. He was just eight years old. The school was founded by a collective of followers of Dr. Ron Maulana Karenga of the US Organization—an organization of extreme activism for the collective rights of African Americans. I had no former knowledge of who these people were. Fortunately, one of the master teachers lived in the same apartment complex as me. We became friends and gathered frequently for Friday-night tacos at my apartment. I learned of the philosophy and practices of communal living among some of the teachers and leaders. Many of the founding families lived in Pasadena, California. The Kawaida Educational Center moved out of Los Angeles and relocated to Pasadena, California. The following year, I enrolled my son in a Christian school.

My son, in his seasoned adult life, shared with me how unsettling it was for him to move from the comfort and stability and safety of his paternal grandparents' care and protection. Moving from small town Vallejo, California, to a metropolitan center of Los Angeles, California, was a culture shock on many fronts. He said he felt secure in his small community of family and friends in Vallejo. Being uprooted from a quiet, secluded community with small public schools to step into the fast-moving currents of schools; then to step into the fast-moving currents of social justice activism, proved to be a big social adjustment for my son and I. I'm very proud of my son. It would be his calm and easy temperament that played a strong role in keeping me grounded first as mother and advocate. The atmosphere was filled with militant and angry voices and chants of justice now in every aspect of society. In May 1973, my son and I stepped into the loud, boisterous, and sometimes threatening climate of social justice change in Los Angeles, California. Within a year, one of my co-workers encouraged me to get a gun. Uneasy at the thought of doing self-harm, I disposed of it the following year.

Reflections

Reflecting, rereading and rewriting sections of this chapter kept me uneasy and hesitant to step back into my past. I wanted to quickly hurry and complete my edits with little emotional drama as possible. But my paraclete, my Holy Spirit, had different plans for me. Plans to take me by the hand, reach back and down in those hurtful places and heal and deliver me in a special and intimate way. I knew I needed to call on my circle of friends and family to uphold me in prayer. I wanted help getting clarity and different perspectives on what it was like for them to witness certain traumatic events in my life. One friend referred to the character as controlling. Another said we were afraid for you and son. Looking back, surely this was a love affair gone wrong. "Sometimes we allow our emotions to run wild without engaging our heads, says author Linda Hollies in her book, Jesus and Those Bodacious Women." This was my story on way too many occasions.

Before getting still, I paced to and from my computer for several days. Listening for God to instruct me on how to begin my deliverance process. Each morning I would plug into the soothing piano worship music by Dappy Keys to help me settle down. Prompted by the Holy Spirit, I reached out to one of my BGU graduate degree professors, Dr. Wes Johnson—incredible spiritual director and soul care expert. Wes was my 2010 spiritual guide into the inner healing benefits of contemplative prayer methods at the five-day Reflective Prayer Retreat. When we connected, he had clear recall of my inner-healing breakthrough during the five-day retreat. He encouraged me to involve my community in my remembering. Like Mary, mother of Jesus, she had the disciples and others to lean on to help her process the trauma of watching her son and her Savior hang, bleed and die on the Cross at Calvary.

Reminded that I was equipped with inner healing tools from various resources I've used over the years, I began revisiting and reviewing self-help books and contemplative prayer methods. I surrendered to His steadfast love and a safe way that would soon release me from harboring unforgiveness and shame. Holy Spirit apprehended me for nearly forty days during chapter five edits. I was moved and led by the Spirit to trust Him as I spent intentional time remembering, in mindful meditation, and recalling and repenting of the sordid events of my past. Aching memories that had kept me emotionally hostage for over forty-plus years. It was time for me to come clean with myself and with my caring community about my hidden angst of fear, shame, bitterness, feelings of unworthiness, and unforgiveness.

In humble submission to the ancient process of Lectio Divina, breath prayer, and armed with selective Scriptures, I sat on my porch and engaged in the memory of the pain. Facing my fears and past sins, warm tears would flow down my cheeks. There were days when the Spirit would quicken me to ask for and speak forgiveness over individuals who brought hurt and harm over my life (whether living or dead). Inspired with confidence to write from a place of transparency and forgiveness, I began to put pen to paper with courage and blessed assurance that Christ would be my guide, protector, and healer as I looked back into my young unsettled life. This time I would take hold of Jesus hand, pressing close to him, and yielding to the good Shepherd and Comforter. He would lead me through the valley of the shadow of hurtful memories. Into the way of lasting peace.

Forgiveness

How does one develop the capacity to forgive? A message by a television evangelist sheds the light on Jesus as the example. Jesus is hanging on the cross between two thieves. Jesus the Christ appeals to the Father in prayer, not to remove him from the situation but to please change the minds of those who did not know or believe that Jesus was the Christ, the Son of the living God. Forgiveness is a continuous process. It would take nearly forty years before my heart would be made ready to forgive others and ultimately forgive myself. It would take nearly forty years for me to grasp and grapple with Jeremiah 1:5 before I would get blessed assurance that my life matters. Every step I have taken has been overseen by my Lord and Savior Jesus Christ. Even though I grew up enduring hardships and becoming a teen parent during a time of incredible violence, I learned that my life matters to God my Maker. What a radical affirmation to be known before you were even a thought or seed in your mother's womb.

Who knew my Lord would take these early life experiences and forty-plus years of wilderness training and begin shaping and forming a mighty love within me to advocate for disenfranchised and vulnerable children? Who knew that my steps would be ordered and transformed as I stepped into the climate of radical servants at Bakke Graduate University? Only He knew that Dr. Randy White's book *Encounter God in the City: Onramps to Personal and Community Transformation* would impact my urban-ministry calling in a profound—a calling that would later take me on travels to places like Soweto, South Africa, Chennai, India and to the United Nations to join my voice with voices of other child advocates from many nations around the globe. Most importantly, I give thanks to God for the prayers of the righteous, wise elders past and present. To my ancestry who set an example of prayer advocacy. They left a legacy that battles are first fought and won in prayer. I acknowledge and honor the voices that called my name, moved heaven on my behalf.

It would take all of forty plus years for me to get clarity on the purpose of the Cross and the benefits of the triumphant victory of Christ's Resurrection. There were many times I questioned if his death and resurrection were in fact for me to enjoy the benefits of my salvation on this side of heaven. Shame, guilt and condemnation were constant companions that kept me doubting my worthiness. Much later in life I would realize the pure and holy Blood that Jesus shed for me, was not just an event. He left heaven and the comfort of his Deity on my behalf. He died in my place—a perfect substitute. Fulfilling the promise of redemption and resurrection, he rose from the grave on the third day. Thus, making it possible for me to be risen from my painful past memories and sin sick soul. He welcomes me back into the safety of the Family of God. What radical love.

Joy on the journey. This healing and writing journey did not end with confronting and taking the terror out of the traumatic events of my past. My renewed courage put me on path to experience the power and victorious living as a result of His obedience to the Father and the power of his resurrection. An inner strength and hope like no other filled me with shalom and acceptance with God. I felt at home. Shame and condemnation could no longer keep me feeling left out. Shame had me believing that not even God wanted me. But the message and power of redemption overrides every condemning thought of the enemy.

In his book, My Grandmother's Hands, author Menekem, captures my before and after soul makeover with these words, "God is the ultimate lover, who chases us when we had nothing to offer. This love came our way, when we were downright ugly, dirty, filthy, and lost in our sin. When we were in the gutter of life, God came and picked us up, turned us around, and claimed us with His love." What manner of love is this! How radical is that!

"As sons and daughters of the Second Adam, we can once again enjoy long walks in the Garden with our God. Because of the resurrection we have the power to overcome the brokenness caused by sin… and renewal of his image in our lives and in all our relationships…" (Reflective Prayer Retreat 2010).

Remembering the saints who prayed for me. I salute those who prayed for me while I was in the desert of life. My ancestors and wisdom of the elders of my time. My grandmothers, great grandmothers, and all the mothers who gave voice to my name, and moved heaven on my behalf. I give thanks with a grateful heart, especially to my son Frank for his enduring faith, patiently waiting on his mother's inner healing and transformation.

Chapter Five is Dedicated to My Son Frank

Chapter 6

Desperate for Change

Faith is taking the first step even when you
don't see the whole staircase.
—Martin Luther King Jr.

Yes, I was a hot mess and rebellious too! It was frightening to leave
in this way. But I believed the Lord shone his light on me as a live-
or-die moment. The message was clear. If I did not completely sever
and leave the unsafe and unprotected lifestyle I was living before my
son, I would surely die. This event became the turning point for me
to choose a different path, make a big change.

Change on the Horizon

The demands and protests of the 1960s civil rights movement
opened doors of economic justice to many of my friends and siblings and to me. By 1970 San Francisco financial district had become
the door by which we in hopes of gaining meaningful and sustaining employment. We were not properly oriented or trained for the
cultural shock of workplace isms. Therefore, employment agencies
were established as a point of referral and a quick orientation to skills
needed at the time.

I recall an interview with an employment agency. The insurance
company was looking for a clerk who had experience typing notes

from recorded equipment and who could work a telephone switchboard. My introduction and training to the use of this piece of equipment was simply "the pedal on the left is for rewind, and the pedal on the right is to go forward." Young girls like me were happy to become a part of the fabric of the work world of America. I was interviewed and was hired. It still amazes me today how the process of orientation and training, although brief, provided me with access to corporate America. Is there any genius in this aspect of my development? I say God's grace was and is at work in all my steps.

By now, my son's father was out of control. He later informed me that from the age of eighteen to thirty-five, he was using and dealing drugs. He was living an addictive and irresponsible lifestyle before his children and me but mostly before his mother and God. He had entered the dark world of drug sales and drug use, along with the crimes associated with such an illegal and unsavory industry. In addition, he had planted his seed whenever a fertile womb would allow.

Today my son interacts well with four siblings of four different mothers. They all communicate and fellowship to some degree in Vallejo. I remember a question my son asked when he was just about six years old: "Why does my father promise to do things with me and never show up?" His words pricked my heart, for not only was his father not there for him but was also not there for me as a parent. In that instance, God spoke to my heart to not speak any words of discord that would further damage my son's heart concerning his father. I was compelled to give a soft answer like, "He means well, and he will do better the next time." I knew there would not be a next time. I knew a change was coming soon. I just didn't know its magnitude. My heart shifted from speaking negatively over the life of my son's father to asking God to deliver him from drugs and create in him a clean heart for the sake of his children.

Frank Earl, my son's father, gives credit to God for keeping and saving his life. He gave his life to Christ while incarcerated. Today Frank Earl lives a drug-free life at seventy-one. He has a thriving landscaping business and proudly says, "Now I can serve my children and their children." Further, he says he works to ensure that when his grandchildren make a request of him, he's in a position to provide. Now that's radical!

Throughout this writing endeavor, I have been reading a collection of Maya Angelou's autobiographies. What I find so interesting and parallel to my story are her stories of trials and triumphs, of becoming a teen mother, and with transparency, of seeking significance in her relationships or the right combination of people and places to bring her joy as daughter, mother, dancer, singer, lover, wife, and activist. Although she was born in 1928, I saw some striking occurrences. I was born in 1948. Like Maya, I, too, was pregnant at age sixteen. Like Maya, I, too, was struck by the looks and was deceived into relationships with men with ill intentions. Like Maya, I lived and worked in San Francisco and Oakland, California, hoping to discover myself. Like Maya, when my son was still under age fourteen, we moved several times between Vallejo, Oakland, and Los Angeles. Although he was in the best hands of his paternal grandparents, like Maya, I was absent from my son more often than I desired to be.

What were the times calling for in our minds and hearts? What was this move on our souls in search of? Was it just related to the new release of hormones that we knew not of? Or was the divine at work calling and navigating in some unique way unfamiliar and unknown to us?

Desperate for You

After giving notice to my employer, KCBS Radio Station at One Embarcadero Center, I packed up my feeble life and belongings in my little 1971 yellow Volkswagen and drove southbound on Interstate 5. With just a phone number and a pouting eight-year-old son, I was determined to live a safer life, a better one than I was leaving. There were many betrayals I needed to work out. Away from questionable family and friends. I could feel a strong, desperate desire to live. *What aspect of my character was in need of a divine touch?* I was desperate for the Lord. I felt out of reach of my Lord. Or was I still rebelling?

In the midst of great emotional, social, and political upheaval, this vulnerable single mother of an African American male child uprooted her life from little town Vallejo to the swiftly moving currents of community activism. Unbeknownst to me, I had entered the bedrock of community involvement on a grand and formal scale than I could comprehend. I quickly learned to blend my voice in with other angry, oppressed voices of change, demanding justice for all.

Social Justice in Action

Teen Post Youth Information Center was a grassroots culture of agents of change. I was being fast-tracked in various streams of social action programs and initiatives: social-political, law enforcement, faith-based and community-based organizations, including the dynamics of fitting in with a team well versed in community involvement response.

A year later, I would be recommended to participate in an innovative, high performing public affairs training program through The Liaison Citizens Training Program.

We were often referred to as the motley crew by those who thought more highly of themselves than they ought. The executive director was a man of many second chances and lots of grace from God. Lonnie Wilson (deceased) was a former alcoholic, an ex-drug addict, an ex-offender of many misdemeanors, an ex-husband, and more. He had an incredible gift of gab and street talk and ability to enter into a courtroom or ballroom and bring good intention and laughter to the downtrodden and to those who thought themselves to a standard or two above others. He could spot a traumatized victim whether dressed up or dressed down. Once in his smooth talking but safe embrace, your life would take on a different kind of hopefulness. I watched and learned.

The Teen Post street team watched and learned how to draw a gang member, a drug user, a low reader, or an unwanted child into our grasp for the sake of saving them from further devastation. This work experience was my introduction to helping the poor at a surreal, grassroots level. Later my attempt at trying to save everyone took its toll on my well-being. It would take years, but I eventually learned that the matters of the oppressed and poor were well beyond my capacity to save them. Jesus is the only Savior.

When I began with Teen Post, Inc., Valerie Shaw, Greg English, Greg Chambers, Lonnie Mayfield, Marlon Bishop, Tyrone Holmes, Gloria Lloyd, Charlotte Tysen, and others made up the core group of the Teen Post community team that served South Los Angeles youth well. Each one brought unique skill sets to the table. The diversity of talents and abilities differed in intellectual capital and as well as the streetwise ex-offender. Teen Post Inc. attracted local professional volunteers and graduate interns. After the 1965 Watts Riots, studies of human behavior and poverty were flowing steadily through South Los Angeles. Teen Post was quite often a site of academic investigation—from the affluent graduate school to the illiterate ex-gang member, from family law judges to social workers—and was often a drop-by site for political campaign candidates.

The Teen Post Youth Information Center experience covered my son and I with love and protection. And some pretty bold on-the-ground living examples of social action in unforgettable ways. It helped us forge relationships.

With the least, last, and lost we developed street smarts; participated in radical public speaking forums, and organized peaceful protests. At times, our street team would be first responders to public safety issues involving gang violence and civil unrest among the poor and under-resourced communities in some incredible and compassionate ways. I quickly learned that I could trust this team to have my back when we were called to assist with keeping peace in the neighborhood.

Within three years, many social and economic resources opened doors of home ownership, access to educational advancements, professional training, and plenty of cultural arts, recreation and theater, for my son and I. We had a home, place of refuge, with a back yard and front porch too. I could exhale.

LORETTA B. RANDLE, M.A.

Social Justice Preparation

The Liaison Citizen Training Program

"A community based training program in the field of public affairs" 1974-75

After the Watts Riots of 1965, charitable and federally funded programs offered residents in underserved communities with tangible resources to equip, educate and empower them to participate as involved citizens in the ebb and flow and discipline of becoming constructive, active and self-governing citizens in society. It would be the recommendation of the executive director of Teen Post Youth Information Center for me to participate in the Liaison Citizen Training Program. My servant leadership development went into tactical development through this program. My advocacy and community activism skills were being perfected in ways I did not fully comprehend at the time. Looking back, I can see the Lord's hand strengthening and reconstituting my internal capacity. Capturing my angry voice and putting it to good use for the sake of the underserved. I was becoming His radical servant leader.

The Liaison Citizen Training Program is unique in its design and delivery, and marketing. W. Don Fletcher (deceased)founder of LCTP, and former co-founder of CORO Fellows Foundation, believed that genius and intellectual capital existed in and among diverse, and larger numbers of people and places. Those who were intentionally left out of decision-making processes of government and of society. Especially within the African American culture and communities. The LCTP, a course in Public Affairs, developed my capacity in community involvement. We were trained to seek to understand how key decision-makers weigh issues that they encounter.

LCTP developed teams of skilled citizens. Trained in the art and science of interviewing and discovery. We were coached to listen, analyze, and to communicate ideas, and to collaborate effectively within a group. Through discussions, socials, role plays, seminars we understood our leadership potential was under development. Then, LC trainees would put to work what we had learned. To culminate LC trainees' efforts, a field trip to the state capital afforded the opportunity to interview legislators, administrators, lobbyists and media representatives on the state level.

Through a federal mandate the Resident Citizens Training Program was launched to reach underserved and disenfranchised citizens. Offerings were available to African American residents to improve, increase and strengthen their education and career-ladder successes, including access to home ownership. Community colleges and four-year colleges created college government supported entrance programs to receive the new student population. I enjoyed the benefit of completing my A.A. degree at Los Angeles Southwest College. A few years later, these same supports enabled me to complete my B.A degree from University of Redlands.

However, my soul and spirit were thirsty for righteousness. My behavior remained promiscuous. I was not completely there for my son during those critical adolescent years. Community events and other disadvantaged youth became my priority. Even so, in doing well, I remained ashamed. I would come home from work with no meal plan for my son, so McDonald's became a weekly source of dinner in our household. I remember having a meltdown when my son was about age sixteen. I was tired of the search-and-rescue mentality that was driving me to serve. I was not the Savior. But I did not know how to put the brakes on my overtaxed emotions and soul. My son grabbed me and said it was going to be all right. In that moment, I knew my son had become a man.

My passion for justice and advocacy for vulnerable children began to take on a larger-than-life burden. Frank was on the verge of not graduating from high school on time. He was naturally smart and very perceptive. He was gregarious and thoughtful. His teachers loved him throughout his elementary journey. They each commented on his potential of leadership giftedness. He was a thinker and observer of people and their actions, and he would make small notes and comments of such.

At age ten, my son and a grade school friend took the important walk down the long aisle of First AME Church and accepted Jesus Christ into their heart. At age eleven, he was the sixth-grade class-graduation spokesperson. On both of these occasions, I was so proud. When I look back over these events, it puts a smile in my heart. Frank was adapting and making adjustments to new people, new schools, new culture, and more; and he was doing so with a warm smile. Thank you, Jesus, for your keeping grace.

It was of the utmost priority to find a local church for my son and I. As God would have it, within the first year of my relocation to Los Angeles, I would meet a wise old woman we called "Mama Smith." My employment in Los Angeles began with Teen Post Youth Information Center in Watts, September 1973. TPYIC was a nonprofit youth development organization. One of its outreach programs included drug education and prevention, including gang intervention services. It was customary for the City of Los Angeles Youth Employment Program to partner with local faith and community-based organizations to operate as host agencies for neighborhood youth to participate in annual eight-week employment and character enrichment activities. A federal mandate initiated after the tumultuous riots and civil unrest of 1965.

As summer youth worker program coordinator, I was fast-tracked and oriented to cultural norms and programs that were offered to at risk youth each summer. Free and selective movie showings were included as a compliment to underserved youth in South Los Angeles. My first encounter with this type of active community engagement took place at the Los Angeles Police Department Parker Center Auditorium. A place and space strategy of local law enforcement to control and contain community violence. Through agency collaboration, hundreds of youths would get the chance to experience movies intended to enrich and motivate the minds of youth we served. It would be in this context that I would meet and become quickly acquainted with, and embraced by Mrs. Geraldine "Mama Smith" Scott, music and choir director of First A.M.E. church.

Wisdom of the elders are necessary liaisons. Especially when you are young, unexperienced and unaware, particularly in a new and unfamiliar region and cultural landscape.

When we met, Mama Smith she was already an older adult. A graduate of Howard University, with a degree in Music. Mama Smith used her gifts and talents as an outreach effort to connect to the rag, tag and poor. Through El Roi eyes, she saw me. Within minutes she quickly apprehended my soul to meet her at the next choir rehearsal at First A.M.E. Church in Los Angeles. FAME, as the church is affectionately referred, has a long, rich historical presence as a social action African American church. My son and I were embraced as her extended family. Whew! I was so happy to make her acquaintance. Personally, I needed an older adult in my life who loved Jesus and would be a positive role model too. She was feisty and bold enough to speak life into my desolate and shameful soul. For the next ten years, through the art of music and community engagement Mama Smith had me and my son in tow of her five choirs. She taught us all forms of voice control and movement. She was extreme in her vocal coaching practices. Her choirs were well known in California. We sang at special events throughout the city and the state. Mama Smith was well connected to various influencers in the entertainment, arts and political arena. Connecting and engaging her choir members in diverse cultural venues was her gift and passion. Not only did I now have a church home for my son and I, we had friends and a community of caring individuals to help us thrive.

IN MEMORY OF Geraldine "Mama Scott Smith"

Chapter 7

A Culture of Radical Servant Leaders

Most assuredly, I say to you the Son can do nothing of
Himself, but what He sees the Father do, for whatever
He does, the Son also does in like manner.

—John 5:19

According to Mark 10:45, "Jesus came to serve, not to be served."
This is the way and life of the Bakke clan, of Dr. Lowell Bakke in
particular, and the roster of a multicultural, multinational, and multigenerational lineup of professors, staff, and student comrades.

Synonymous with the word or idea of servant is giving. In the
purpose and example of the life of Jesus Christ is his act of giving
himself away. "He gives to all mankind life and breath in everything…" (Acts 17:25). He shows us how to serve by giving ourselves
away so that he is glorified. Believers are called first by God and
confirmed in service by his words, "Whoever serves [speaks]…serves
by the strength that God supplies [abundantly…in everything], so
that God may be glorified through Jesus Christ [the Messiah]." (1
Pet. 4:11)

On my arrival to Seattle, Washington, on February 2010, Dr.
Lowell Bakke and wife, Diana, opened their hearts and home to me
to stay overnight before my first course, a five-day prayer intensive,
which began the next morning. This is the way the culture of servants living out their gospel calling in a real and tangible way should

begin. I would soon learn that the Bakke clan includes people who are servants first in everything that they do and say, including the way they interact with their families, callings, and communities.

My heart leaps at the joy of learning servant leadership philosophy with Bakke professors Grace, Judi, John, Lowell, Nancy, and Wes, as each one creatively and prophetically engaged and enlivened the Word of God.

Who is Bakke?

Bakke Graduate University (BGU) is the story of a family of radical servants of God. Ray Bakke, leader of Lausanne Urban Associates; brother Dennis Bakke, founder of AES (largest independent electricity company in the world); brother Lowell Bakke, an innovative pastor; and sister Marilyn Bakke Pearson, a gifted Bible teacher.

Originally named the Northwest Graduate School of Ministry (NWGS) in 1990. A survey of over 70 key leaders in the Lausanne Committee for World Evangelization originally formed by Billy Graham in 1960 demonstrated an overwhelming global need for a new type of education. What was missing was ways to apply theology to massive trends of urban migration, the growth of global cities, the rise of economics and business as the new center of influence for the gospel. As a result, Bakke Graduate University became the new school. It was designed to have three colleges of Christian theology, urban studies, and business with students studying together. BGU mission is to strengthen leaders who steward resources with and for vulnerable people and places, by means of contextual, Christian-based education innovatively delivered throughout the urban world. (https://bgu.edu/about/university-profile/#Our%20Story)

Dr. Ray Bakke's book *A Theology as Big as the City* reveals his calling, which is to unpack and reveal God's love for all people. He does so in a marvelously unique way as expressed in his book and his many roles and positions he has occupied in the Christian community locally and globally. One profound takeaway from his book is that the theology of men must become more compassionate with a greater, bigger, and wider reach to capture the socioeconomic justice of all people—rich and poor, immigrant and citizen, regardless of one's station or status in life. Jesus walked, lived, and ministered to all people. Jesus was acquainted with all our schisms.

Dr. Grace Barnes, another excellent example of a profound servant leader, did an exceptional job of providing instruction in the prescribed coursework of servant leadership. The context of my life of service to humanity fit ever so sweetly within this transformational leadership perspective. She guided my thought process through her written book on *Servant First*. With volumes of books, articles, and other material and through the power of the Holy Spirit, I was able to expand my understanding of out-of-the-box ways to serve God and frame my transformational context of service with biblical and practical teaching and doctrine that works. Dr. Grace is my servant-leader advocate, mentor, and eternal friend. She continues to nudge my soul to allow the best of Jesus Christ to shine through my gifts and talents, specifically as a writer. It has been her constant and steady presence by regular telephone sessions confirming and midwifing this book-writing endeavor to life.

Dr. Judi Melton is an incredible servant of God. Not only does she hold the office of registrar but she also actually became the glue, the compassion that held me steady and on course to complete my degree. Midway through my degree-completion timeline, I became very ill. I called Judi, and she immediately put protocol and processes in place to hold my degree work in place. Not only that, she also sensed my lack of personal worth and damaged emotions and little confidence to step boldly into a culture of highly trained and disciplined servant leaders. So the Holy Spirit used her to woo me with her gentle and reassuring voice to trust Jesus and to continue to press into this loving culture of caring servants.

It would be the words of Barack Obama, the first African American President of the United States, serving in the highest public servant's office in America, that motivated me and many of its citizens to return or go to school. I took the leap and did just that. So at the age of sixty-two, thoughts of my future hinged on President Obama's words for the people to take action and develop a "yes, I can" attitude. My employment with World Vision had a global layoff in the winter of 2007. Just two years prior to the layoff, I had cancer surgery. By 2008, I was unemployed and found it very difficult to reenter the workforce as an older adult. By 2009, my financial security was severely challenged, so I thought, *Why not go back to school?* I made an inquiry into Bakke Graduate University and was soon enrolled in the Master of Arts in Global Urban Leadership program. Why BGU? During my employment with World Vision, BGU had a Christian leaders training and development partnership with World Vision US Programs. At the time, BGU was named Northwestern University.

Servant leadership is one of BGU's eight transformational leadership perspectives that frame all its graduate programs. Author Greenleaf believes before you can be a leader, you must first be a servant.

> It begins with the natural feeling that one wants to serve first. Then conscious choice brings one to aspire to lead. It is not about being servile, it is about wanting to help others. It is about identifying and meeting the needs of colleagues, customers, and communities.

Now his perspective touched a deep cord within me. This idea flipped my intellectual script and professional leadership development. Never had the two themes of servant and leader intersected. In my role as associate director of training in leadership development at United Way Kellogg Training Center, emphasis was placed on becoming the best volunteer leader. One of America's core values. Greenleaf's philosophy, towards the practice of servant leadership, grounded me in thought and deed. I felt a strong willingness to make an intentional character strength shift. My soul said yes to servant leader. His theory and practice grounded me in thought and deed and willingness to make a divine and well-intended change in mind, soul, and spirit. I heard myself saying yes to servant leader.

This makes sense. This is the way of Christ. As our King, He served humanity first. How radical is Jesus's servant leadership!

I had stepped into a steady stream and current of innovative, creative coursework within the Bakke culture. My first class was first listed as servant leaders. It was cancelled. Dr. Lowell Bakke immediately suggested a five-day prayer retreat: Reflective Prayer and Biblical Meditations coupled with a retreat theme of "Come Away and Be Still." It was directed and facilitated by Dr. Wes Johnson—an incredible theologian, an excellent practitioner of contemplative prayer methods, a writer, and a storyteller. My whole being would become so strengthened by an aspect of his dissertation theme: "Lectio Divina for Busy People." Boy, did I need to get away and get still.

My life was undergoing a major overhaul. My emotional and financial health were a blistering mess. It was January 2010, and no employment income was in sight since December 2007. My savings were being depleted. My home was in and out of the threat of foreclosure. I was tapping into my retirement funds to just make ends meet. My friends and local church were getting a little short with me, as I was asking for help almost quarterly for most of 2009 to 2010. One even demanded that I go and get a job and stop withdrawing from my retirement investments. Mind you, at the time, I was age sixty. Mainstream workforce was not so user-friendly toward older adults.

My calls to and from Lowell and Judi were handled with a spirit of compassion and gentleness. They perceived and understood how emotionally fragile I was during this time of transition. I was not turned away. Rather, I was sweetly embraced into a culture of kind-hearted servant leaders. There was a kindred spirit among us. Surely Christ was the glue.

God's mission was becoming clearer and I was getting laser focused about the perfecting work necessary to innovate my capacity to "Go ye therefore…into the cities" (Matt.28:19). Thus, my journey into a different cultural understanding of transformation leadership perspectives had begun.

It was Super bowl Sunday, February 2010. I was on a plane from Los Angeles, CA to Seattle, WA. While in flight, and in preparation of my first BGU course, I was making an intentional effort to speed read and grasp hold to the key concepts and principles of breath prayer, centering prayer and Lectio Divina. Dr. Wes Johnson had written about these contemplative prayer themes in his 492-page dissertation, "Experiencing God's Transforming Presence: Praying His Names in the High Points and Low Points of Life." Other required reading included one book in particular that sparked a light and inner dialogue within my soul: *Let Your Life Speak.* I was intrigued by the thought that the life of Christ within me was speaking ever so gingerly, purposely, and consistently. I yielded to this new awareness of engaging the Spirit of God. I became still and quiet and began to trust the divine conversation and exchange. It was okay for me to enjoy this invisible, divine presence with my questions, thoughts, ideas, and dreams. This practice of listening to my inner life speak brought joy to my spirit and soul. This was a new spiritual and soulful place and space of being with my Lord and Savior. BGU coursework challenged me to settle my soul down and learn to listen in on what the Spirit was saying to me.

Dr. Lowell Bakke met me at the airport in Seattle, WA. He phoned me just as I was de-boarding the plane. After arriving to his home and meeting his lovely wife, Diana, we had a light meal and chatted for a while. A selfcare hobby of mine is providing wellness supports of hand and foot spa to those in service to others. A hand spa was provided to Diana. My way of saying thank you for opening their hearts and home to me. I slept lightly. Early the next morning Lowell drove me further north to Everett, WA to connect with Dr. Wes Johnson, professor and spiritual director in charge of the five-day prayer intensive course, and his lovely wife Kathryn. As they drove, both Lowell and Wes shared and delighted to tell of their cultural history and the social and economic transitions of their cities and townships.

Cedar Springs Retreat Center was an unknown place to me. The Canadian border was just a stone's throw beyond the retreat center. I was on my way to meet some unknown people (BGU students) from Washington State and Toronto, Canada, and surrounding cities. It would be here where I would encounter the transforming work and presence of God Himself—in an unknown way through unfamiliar coursework that included the practice of Lectio Divina.

Once I stepped onto the property of Cedar Springs my breath was taken by the luminous Cedar trees and acre upon acre of a beautifully, well-manicured landscape, including the clipped wings of the Swans gently floating on the peaceful lake. It felt a little like heaven.

The innovatively designed and thoughtfully delivered courses of BGU were inviting, and equally challenging in helping me to settle my soul down to listen in on what the Holy Spirit was saying. The art of practicing Lectio Divina provided me with profound and incredible, transforming lessons in deep callings. The Lectio Divina process began to illuminate the presence and love of Christ at work within me. Whew! This was so radical! I had no idea I could experience such closeness and intimacy with God the Father through this method and discipline of being still. Professor Wes was well able, equipped and guided us with much empathy and compassion.

What is Lectio Divina

Within 30 minutes of our arrival at Cedar Springs, Professor Wes began the first lesson in Lectio by diving right into the reading of Psalm 131.

He introduced elements of the contemplative process and shared how we will start with stories of living in the moment through creating a personal timeline with high points and low points in our life. Professor Wes shared his role as not only teacher but spiritual director, with emphasis on listening to the Holy Spirit as he listens to the participants.

He provided instruction in theological foundations of praying the events of life, along with sharing the history of our desert fathers—early Christian hermits whose practice of asceticism (a lifestyle of abstinence) in the Egyptian desert, beginning in the third century, formed the basis of Christian monasticism.

In Western Christianity, Lectio Divina is a traditional monastic practice of scriptural reading, meditation and prayer intended to promote communion with God and to increase one's knowledge of

God's Word. It does not treat scripture as text to be studied, but as the living word. Believers who chose to go into the desert as hermits were said to be answering the call of Christ. (https://en.wikipedia. org/wiki/Lectio Divina)

Professor Wes directed our attention to Deuteronomy 8:10-18 and Joshua 4:6-7; each passage gives stories of God's activities in man's story, and shows key events of high points and low points and how the people overcame. Moreover, he gave insight into the biblical stories and how God's story is at work in the work of a leader. He seals the introduction in my soul with these words, "The foundation for Lectio is shaped by God's Word and is a good and practical spiritual formation tool that allows Lectio to read our soul." We were encouraged to remember those who mentioned our name during high and low points in life. Even to remember the desert generation who failed in their wanderings (Moses and the children of Israel). We are to look back at our past failures and learn from them. We are to remember our leaders and consider their outcomes—especially Jesus who is our best leader. We are to hold fast to the value of Christ.

The next sentence that flowed out of his mouth was like a parting of the red sea of my soul. I began to tear as he spoke: "Lectio is sitting with God who has moved all of Heaven and earth to be with you." My shameful sinful life had kept me feeling I was not wanted. But just in the first hour of our session my spirit and soul were being watered, refreshed and renewed. The Creator of the universe had navigated my travels to such a place as this, for such a time as this. I was affirmed as His Beloved. The day had been long, yet, enriching and inspiring. Rivers of living waters were flowing from my heart to my hand as I wrote in my journal. It was nearly midnight before I put the pen down. It was my first night away. I slept well.

Reflections

Looking back over my BGU coursework, I can see how this one course had better equipped me for the encounters of humility I would need in my own soul as I am called in service to others. I recall a pre-course teleconference with Dr. Lowell Bakke where he put into perspective the language of transformation leadership. He said something to the effect of, "You will learn new ways of expressing God's love through your life experiences." Those words became a reality in my called life as an ambassador of Christ. It was as though I had learned a new language. No longer a silent sufferer an option for me. The contemplative practice of Lectio Divina and the other courses that followed, had revealed the life of Christ speaking within me, strengthening me to learn to live and love out loud, unashamedly, with boldness in Truth.

Five days and four nights of deep abiding soul care. I was strengthened in my inner woman. I arrived with a blank slate, an empty (depleted) vessel. I returned home with a banquet full of spiritual entrees to use in my daily communion with the Lord. And to share with my family, friends, and community leaders.

Professor Wes charged me to return to my community. Inform, teach and share what I had learned. I was to seek out busy people; children, students, adults, executives, and those living in busy urban places like Los Angeles, CA, Oakland, CA and Sacramento, CA. He did a great work at equipping me to equip others in this remarkable, transformative, and inner healing practice of listening in on the internal conversation that the Spirit of God was having on the inside of my soul. I learned the discipline and value of sitting with Scripture and allowing Scripture to read my soul. I left the retreat very encouraged to allow the good work begun in my soul to now be revealed as a lifestyle.

There would be plenty more of innovative BGU coursework that would take Christianity and Christ out of the box. Kingdom Narratives, taught by Professor John Lewis, Jesus at Work, Christian Community Development and Advocacy, and volumes of books on how and ways to transform lives and places and spaces where hurting people live.

Dedicated to the Radical Servant Leaders
of Bakke Graduate University

Chapter 8

The Transforming Power of Eight

> Samuel anointed David, the eighth son...
>
> —1 Samuel 16:12

Eight in the Bible symbolizes the beginning of new things. Boys were to be circumcised on the eighth day. The number 8 symbolizes the circumcision of the heart through Christ and the receiving of the Holy Spirit (Rom 2:28–29; Col 2:11–13). "Those in Christ are becoming a new creation, with godly character being created by the power of God's Spirit" (2 Cor 5:17; Eph 2:10, 4:23–24). (http://www.biblestudy.org/bibleref/meaning-of-numbers-in-bible/8.html).

God the Creator saved eight people after the flood to begin a new world and new life. In the Old Testament biblical times boys were circumcised on the eighth day. The prophet Samuel was told to anoint David, the shepherd boy, to be the next King of Israel. David was the eighth son of Jesse. Jesus showed himself eight times after his resurrection from the dead, and before his ascension to heaven. Although the fourth born, my mother gave birth to me, Loretta B. Randle, the first born in California, August, the eighth month of 1948. A new beginning for the growing Randle clan.

All coursework taught at Bakke Graduate University incorporates eight transformation leadership perspectives. These TL perspectives provide a framework for me to get a broader insight into ways to express meaning and ways the body of Christ could show up in urban settings with the blessed assurance that one is moving in the rhythm and flow of the love of Jesus Christ.

Romans 12:2: "Do not be conformed to this world, but be transformed by the renewing of your minds so that you may discern what is the will of God—what is good and acceptable and perfect." Scripture provides a context and a foundation for believers to get an understanding, and comprehend the process and importance of surrendering to a life of transformation in Christ.

A picture of transformation comes to mind. Imagine the transforming life process a caterpillar goes through at becoming a beautiful, regal butterfly. It begins as a potential meal to birds and other critters. Yet in its call to be transformed, the caterpillar takes measures to begin its metamorphosis. "A caterpillar spends most of its life crawling on—and devouring—its food source. But when it's time to become an adult, most caterpillars start to wander away from what they've been eating. They find a sheltered, safe spot in which to pupate, or transform into an adult.") (https://animals.howstuffworks.com/insects/caterpillar3.htm)

This little caterpillar girl wanted so much at becoming a thriving and flourishing adult—spiritually, physically, and emotionally. After years of "crawling on my belly"—attempting to hide my sinful past, harboring unforgiveness, including feelings of unworthiness. The Caller apprehended my sin sick soul, guiding me to be among people pursuing ways of becoming more Christ like. Awareness of my personal transformation began during a season of systematic Bible study and pastoral care at First Berean Christian Church in the early 1980s. Dr. Sherrill McMillan taught, trained many of the congregants in follow-through evangelism. One training segment focused on strengthening one's ability to remember Bible verses as a tool to witness to others. It would be Romans 12:2…" be ye transformed by the renewing of your mind…," that settle down deep in my soul. It would take years before I would realize that transformation was not a one-time event. It is a lifetime process.

Believers are challenged on a daily basis to resist conforming to thoughts and actions of the world systems, against popular culture and manner of thinking which is in direct rebellion against God. By the moving power of God's Word, I was compelled to change my living arrangements with my live in mate. A couple years later the Holy Spirit strengthened me to stop smoking cigarettes, too. In cooperation with, and not apart from, the central effort of the Holy Spirit, my outward appearances began to reflect my hope and reliance on a holy God to help me prove His good and acceptable will.

During my employ with World Vision US Programs in Los Angeles, His Call confronted me in a most unusual way. My desk calendar offered daily scriptures to reflect on each day. On a particular day, Jeremiah 1:5 loomed off the page and gripped my heart. I thought I could ignore the words..." Before I formed you in the belly, I knew thee..." so I quickly turned to another page. You can run but you can't hide from the God of all Creation. Tentatively, I turned back to the page and read the remaining scripture... "and before thou camest forth out of the womb I sanctified thee, and I ordained thee a prophet unto the nations." Ready or not, when the Caller calls, you will answer. Holy Spirit held fast to my spirit. How could a holy God use a "worm as I" in his mission of redemption of the world. Sarah Youngs, little devotional book, Jesus Calling, put me in closer intimacy with the presence and voice of God in a loving way. The words on each page were like Christ himself was sitting with me, gingerly sharing his heart with me, affirming me as a called servant of his. Twenty years later my understanding of being called as prophet unto the nations has taken on, not so much the office of a prophet, but a spokesperson, a mouth piece of the Kingdom of Heaven. Declaring that Jesus Christ is the way, the truth and the light, unto the least, last and lost. Follow Him.

The Eight Transformation Leadership Perspectives

Calling-based Leadership. BGU describes calling-based leadership as one, a leader, who seeks to understand his/her God-given gifts, experiences, and opportunities in understanding one's unique role as a called instrument of Christ's transforming work in and above world cultures. When I think of examples of calling based leadership in the bible, I am drawn to two characters. Paul, the persecutor of

Christians, called and apprehended on the Damascus Road to later become Apostle Paul. And Mary, called and shrouded by the Holy Spirit for the immaculate conception of Jesus Christ.

At this writing, Russian president Vladimir Putin has declared a special military operation to invade the country of Ukraine. Thirty years ago, a letter of invitation from People-to-People International Citizens Ambassador Program, Women-in-Management Exchange was on my desk at United Way Kellogg Training Center Founded in 1956 by former President Dwight D. Eisenhower as a way to enhance international understanding and friendship through educational, cultural and humanitarian activities. The letter expressed that I would be joined by a multicultural group of women in various leadership/management roles from around the United States. Interviews with women in leadership, working in various industries in Moscow, Ukraine and Kiev, had been scheduled. Fifteen women from various parts of the United States said yes to the Call too.

It would be the connecting flight in Germany to Russia when I realized I was unprepared for the language gap I encountered at the airport. I began to question Did God really call me to take this trip? Would my God allow me to be among potentially untrusting individuals? After all, I was the only African American woman in our group. How would I allow Christ's transforming love show up in this unfamiliar cultural context? Thank God Linda our group leader was waiting for us at the connecting gate. She had our files and pictures in hand. The journey begins.

It would be at a memorial park in Ukraine, remembering the persecuted Jews, where the Caller affirmed my call to be present. There was an incredible sculpture of entangled men, women and children in the center of the entrance to the park. Several of the women expressed they had Jewish ancestors who Hitler ordered to be executed in this place. Prompted by the Holy Spirit I ventured into the park. Encountering a powerful spiritual presence, I humbly backed away and returned to the bus. Surely this was sacred ground. Before taking my sit on the bus the Holy Spirit prompted me to open my mouth. I began making loud declarations of justice and righteousness due African Americans. Later a few women opened up and shared their concerns about the inequities and social ills in America, too. Upon my return home and return to work, I was presented with a termination notice. For nine months, I endured an unlawful termination legal battle. Angry, I cried out, where are you, Lord?

Incarnational Leadership. Described as a leader who pursues shared experiences, shared plights, shared hopes, and shared knowledge and task. In March of 2008 an invitation came through the mail from International Prayer Connect to join forty leaders from various countries for a youth prayer worker consultation in Chennai, India. Just three months earlier I had received notice that the Los Angeles office would be closing. Unemployed again. But God was up to something. Making global cultural connections beyond my grasp. At this season in my life, my heart burns with compassion for at-risk children and families. I submitted my heart and thoughts to the Caller. This time of global travels. I asked my goddaughter, Antonia Jackson to join me. She is an innovator and consultant of youth justice work in Oakland, CA. Both our social justice advocacy callings/gifts were in full view and operation. Showing up and pursuing hurting children and families around the globe became our life style and calling card. During our time in India a visit was organized to meet and greet Father Antone of the Royal Children's Ministry. It would be in this context my calling as an instrument of Christ's transforming work in and above world cultures clarified and seared in my heart. Father Antone's calling is to children who he calls the throw away children. His team goes out and rescues children who have been discarded, left alone, some even to die alone. Trained under the leadership of Mother Teresa, his compassion for the rag, tag and poor kids took my breath. An induction ceremony of new children into the ministry was in progress. In the middle of the process Father Antone invited ministers and pastors sitting in the audience to join him on stage and come and wash the feet of the little ones. It was like I floated to the stage and found myself before a weeping child, washing her feet, and crying too. In that moment I knew the Holy Spirit was present. All of heaven had joined in this moment to affirm and reassure this little one of the love Jesus Christ has for her.

Reflective Leadership. What does it mean to reflect? BGU describes reflective leadership as a leader who lives, in reality, reflects on its meaning and catalyzes others with the courage, symbols, and example to make meaning in their own lives. I was Introduced to the practice of reflective leadership at a prayer retreat. The eyes of my heart were open to a healthier way to engage in deep thought and insight without having a mental health meltdown. A way to engage in non-judgmental dialogue with God, self and others. Reflective leadership became a capacity building skill to use when in group and one-on-one meetings, including service on boards and advisory groups. In my local church context, and while in service on the board of trustees, the act of Biblical reflections was instituted as a prelude before starting board meetings.

Servant Leadership/Contextual Leadership. BGU describes these two-transformation leadership perspective as one whose behavior and priority is on servanthood first. As well as acknowledging previous work of God in other cultures. It would be Dr. Grace Barnes course on servant first that helped me contextualize much of my life experience service to others. Service is what my parents taught and demonstrated before all of my siblings. Spiritually, I was taught to follow community role models in service to humanity. Before encountering the term servant leadership, my acts of service were not grounded in a principle centered way that made natural sense. Required readings and articles on this topic helped me to land my service efforts in a concrete and meaningful way. This transformation leadership perspective caused a shift in my mindset. Two terms, servant and leadership could actually co-exist together and render positive outcomes. Jesus is the role model of servant leadership. Leading by serving. I embraced this principle to enhance my social justice advocacy, integrating it in my lifestyle evangelism presence among family, community and the marketplace.

Strengthened with this leadership perspective, Holy Spirit opened my heart to pursue places and spaces where hurting and vulnerable children and families' dwell. An opportunity to serve girls in foster care became the object of my servant's heart. As of this writing Los Angeles County Department of Children and Family services has over 40,000 open and warm cases. DreamCatcher Foundation, residential care for girls, open its doors to allow me to minister in my unique way. Armed with His servants' heart, the CEO willing gave me access to three group homes for girls. Three days a week I showed up with oranges, a tea kettle, calming music, listening ear and prayer. Later it would be noted, as a result of this wellness intervention the incidence of girls going AWOL (away without leave), running away, was drastically reduced. In this setting I was able to recognize the unique expression of the Gospel in this cultural context. God's footprint was evident as Holy Spirit gave me words to speak life into these fretful and emotionally damaged souls. The Lord affirmed that serving in this way, I was serving the father's will and fulfilling his mission of redemption for the lost among us. Psalm 127:4 remind us that "children are indeed a heritage from the Lord, the fruit of the womb a reward." When we serve the least among us, Heaven opens wide, and is pleased when the souls of one of his little children get to experience a little bit of His glory.

When I reflect on the transformational leadership perspectives of **servant leadership** coupled with **contextual leadership,** I can't help but give thanks to God for the example of Mother Teresa, from obscurity in a small community in Skopje, Macedonia of the region of Greece, to serving the least, last and lost among us in Calcutta, India. To the bold servant leadership of Harriet Tubman. A former African American Slave, and called servant of God to create what is known today as the "Underground Railroad" A human collaboration and passage of escape from American Slavery for hundreds of African Americans. My social justice passion to advocate for all children, especially African American children, can be tied to the historical justice work of Harriet Tubman.

Global Leadership. Los Angeles, CA is a place where the complexities of today's global and pluralistic, urban and socio-economic and political landscape all intersect. Multiple religions and belief system are at play. In general, Churches remain nationalized, denominational, and localized. Social media has opened the window to reach a global audience of believers and non-believers alike. Sunday messages are now heard, seen and forwarded from various applications like Facebook, Instagram, TikTok, WhatsApp, Zoom and other. It is possible that the message of Christ can permeate the mind, body and spirit throughout the world wide web.

When 1000 Grandmother's Pray Prayer Advocacy is an outreach arm of New Visions Christian Fellowship Church in Los Angeles, CA, with a global message of peace and reconciliation. It is rooted in, and acts as a social justice response to vulnerable children and families. Its purpose statement is to mobilize and strengthen the prophetic voices of grandmothers and urban leaders, seek peace for our cities as we covenant vulnerable children in prayer. The ministry has a global presence from Atlanta, GA to Zambia, Africa. Gatherings take place the first Wednesday of each month by Zoom. Four global prayer strategies capture our prayer focus: 1) African American boys reading by nine, thus aborting the pipeline to prison phenomenon,—including sustaining the life of black infants beyond the first year, 2) childhood cancer diagnosis, 3) children separated from birth parents and placed into foster care system, and 4) human sex trafficking of children—all four strategies are a global crisis. In addition, the writer has a thirty-year history of global mission's travel and connections in and between, United States to Russia, Ukraine, Kiev. Including South Africa, Chennai India, and the United Nations.

Shalom. The term, Shalom has a rich historic meaning beyond its media-politicized current characteristics. At best BGU describes this transformation leadership characteristic as the leaders' efforts to pursue reconciling relationships between people, and people and God, and their environment, and people and themselves. The leader works towards the well-being, abundance and wholeness of the community, as well as individuals.

This term has eternal beginnings and endings. The Creator intended that all of his creation to flourish. In Genesis 1:28 ... and God blessed them and God said to them, be fruitful, and multiply, and replenish the earth and subdue it: and have dominion over the fish of the sea, and over the fowl of the air, and over every living thing that moveth upon the earth" ((KJV). The Creator called forth abundance and wholeness to dwell in the midst and among all that He created. In the beginning there was Shalom in the Garden of Eden.

In the book *Not the Way It's Supposed to Be: A Breviary of Sin,* author Cornelius Plantinga described the Old Testament concept of shalom as:

"The webbing together of God, humans, and all creation in justice, fulfillment, and delight is what the Hebrew prophets call shalom. We call it peace but it means far more than mere peace of mind or a cease-fire between enemies. In the Bible, shalom means universal *flourishing:* wholeness and delight—a rich state of affairs in which natural needs are satisfied and natural gifts fruitfully employed, a state of affairs that inspires joyful wonder as its Creator and Savior opens doors and welcomes the creatures in whom he delights. Shalom, in other words, is the way things ought to be."

As I reflect on Shalom as a transformation leadership characteristic and perspective, one word in the authors quote above waters my thirst for a broader and practical understanding—flourish. Upon reviewing several source definitions of the word, my take away is this: strive to live well and joyfully with God and others. Bath relationships in love and nurture a sense of trust in all relationships, especially among and between children. Increase in wisdom and peace with all humanity. Pray for the peace of Israel (and Ukraine). From my personal perspective the spirit and essence of Shalom is to believe the Creator delights in our efforts and courage to reflect his desire for all his creatures to shine and welcome shalom at all times.

Prophetic Leadership. The leader speaks truth with love to and through power of the Holy Spirit. With sacrifice and humility, the leader pursues change in the broken systems and practices in society. Old Testament prophets were used of God as his mouthpiece to speak truth, correction and repentance. Believers are given authority and the right to give voice to those that have no voice (Prov. 31:8-9).

In the spirit of giving voice to the marginalized, least, last and lost among us, the outreach ministry of When 1000 Grandmother's Pray Prayer Advocacy, is organized to strengthen the prophetic voice of the urban leader, to seek peace for our cities and covenant vulnerable children in prayer. Through monthly prayer line gatherings, presence in the boardroom, public comment before Council Chambers, in corporate board rooms, court rooms and the classroom, you will find the prophetic leader speaking truth with love, through the power of the Holy Spirit. In addition, the voices of children are equipped and empowered too. Through the community involvement of Children's Prayer Initiative, young participants are trained to develop and enrich a prayer life that gives them the right to access God directly, and to find favor before decision makers.

Reflections

It's a beautiful peace to know that my calling is a gift of God. Scripture informs and affirms me of my significance in Christ, his servant girl. Transformation Leadership perspectives confirms the value he places on my life, "I will praise thee for I am fearfully and wonderfully made…" (Psa.139:14). Professor Grace Barnes affirmed the gift of calling to be an aspect of one's identity, "The earth is the Lord's and the fulness thereof, the world, and they that dwell therein" (Psa.24:1-2). God's calling sends me, his servant leader, into foreign lands, and among unfamiliar cultures and customs. Contextual leadership, as expressed by BGU, informs my worldview of the power and presence of the Gospel of Jesus Christ in unfamiliar geography and cultures. It has expanded my capacity greatly to look intently and listen attentively for the story of Christ to come alive in other people's places.

The eight Transformation Perspectives encourage me to embrace and hold fast to what God's word says about being in relationship with him and with others. It's the love we have for one another that works and moves believers to reflect the person and character of Jesus Christ. The practice of TL calls for a different approach and a renewed response from the person of Christ. TL perspectives help you to see what and how it is possible to positively impact family and cities, and to incarnate the character of Christ to those he has call us to serve. TL begins in one's own soul. In his book, *Life of the Beloved, author* Nouwen speaks of being and becoming the Beloved. All of the eight TL perspectives provide me with a framework and context to experience an incredible belonging in Christ, and within the Christian community.

Important too, is God's call for believers to be available among vulnerable children in our local urban centers. Older adults show up at places like Girls Club of Los Angeles-Faith Children's Center, Pepperdine University Foster Grandparent Program, including service to the African American Infant Maternal Mortality Initiative. Global outreach includes covenant prayer and support to God Our Help Ministries, Int'l in Lusaka, Zambia Africa. An outreach effort to orphans and families impacted by HIV/Aids.

When I think of servant leader and incarnational leaders, Mother Teresa brings both these perspectives to life. In seeking the Father's will for her life, she was called to go and be among the poorest of the poor in Calcutta, India. Mother Teresa loved Jesus and loved the people He sent her to serve. She served like Jesus. She showed up where hurting people were, whether in high places of leadership or in the lowest segments of a culture. Servant leadership is a more excellent way for one to show up in the world. A way of living and loving out loud in the name of Jesus.

Servant First, as written and articulated by Dr. Grace Barnes, professor of Servant Leadership at BGU, honed my lens and expanded my capacity to serve with greater compassion and gladness. It would be the words of Robert Greenleaf, who encouraged change agents to serve in the boardrooms—don't run from these places of great influence. Be the change within the corporations. Servant leadership is a radical approach to transformation. It would be Dr. Lowell Bakke who left a positive mark on my soul with this phrase. As a leader, a servant leader in the making, I leave you with the same statement that was given to me. "Servant leadership seeks to serve first and ask, how can I help you fulfill the vision the Lord has given you in the role you occupy"?

Dedicated to Dr. Grace and Doug Barnes

Chapter 9

A Course in Transformation

Be still and know that I AM God...
—Psalm 46:1

Let's lectio

Like the little black book of A Course in Miracles, this chapter is my take of a short taste of A Course in Transformation, as prepared and guided by Dr. Wes Johnson. My soul was dry, exhausted and well spent from doing things my way. I was thirsty for a drink of the Living Waters. I was an older adult in her sixties, unemployed, and still in search of my significance. The people had just elected the country's first African American president of the United States of America. Unfortunately, America was experiencing big systems failures. Big financial institutions were buckling under an unstoppable crash. My financial picture was bleak, and so was my personal portfolio. My mortgage company continued to make its daily harassing phone calls. The mortgage lender made its monthly threats of foreclosing on my home. Where was my Lord in all these uncertainties?

It was the kind and generous orthodoxy of Dr. Lowell Bakke that influenced my decision to step into the BGU culture and begin anew. Lowell speaks well of his early Christian formation in servant leadership. He is from a family of innovators of community transformation. I was fascinated with his stories of early leadership empowerment at the hands of his father at the local church. The seed of incarnational leadership was planted early. He remains a good brother and friend in my servant-leadership development journey. He is masterful at assessing, discerning, and assisting in creating the best course fit for his students. I sensed Lowell caught a hold of my emotional and spiritual destitution and lack of vision of my future. He would suggest my first course. It was the title on the flyer that drew me in: "Come Away and Be Still." My soul yearned for peace and stillness. I had become fretful about my financial future. Yet the call to come away was ever so strong. This beckoning moved deeply and lovingly in all my dry places. If this was a new wave of education, then I was all in. I never could imagine an accredited university would have such a thoughtfully crafted and creatively designed curriculum—with inner healing benefits too.

Reflective Prayer for Transformational Leaders, a five-day prayer-retreat intensive, was my entrance in the Bakke Graduate University Master of Arts in Global Urban Leadership program. Little did I know this course would bring deep changes that would heal. It would initiate my intentional personal-transformation process. God was up to something, and I had to go with it. The initial course in which I had registered was Perspectives of Servant Leadership, which was taught by Professor Barnes. However, it was cancelled just weeks before the prayer retreat was to start. With a short window of time to plan and make travel arrangements and work through my fears, I received news that my ninety-year-old godmother had passed away just days before my scheduled departure for Seattle. My travel plans were redirected to fly into Sacramento and assist with funeral arrangements then continue my travels to Seattle, Washington. Once I locked into my seat, a sense of calm swept over me. Maybe it was the many pre-enrollment calls with Dr. Lowell Bakke and Dr. Judi Melton that helped settle my fears of stepping into the BGU culture. So traveling to Seattle, Washington, became another adventure to begin a new path among new people.

In flight, I took out the four-hundred-plus pages of Dr. Wes Johnson's dissertation on "Experiencing God's Transforming Presence: Praying His Names in the High Points and Low Points of Life." Every idea and theme in this huge document was new yet invigorating to me. I did some speed-reading and drank deeply the concept of spiritual disciplines and contemplative prayer methods, like Lectio Divina, breath prayer, timeline, desert fathers, and more. It was required reading before the course began the next day.

Little did I know this creative and innovative course in transformation would bring profound changes that would reconcile my impaired humanity. The coursework brought me to tears and joy of acceptance as I learned the time-honored spiritual disciplines of contemplative prayer methods. The spiritual disciplines were like a refiner's fire, revealing and exposing and removing a lot of stuff that hindered my soul from trusting God and moving out in the steady flow of His abiding love and faithfulness. This chapter shows how God placed my entangled heart on the altar of peace and on a path of redemption and renewal in the context of a course in Reflective Prayer for Transformational Leaders.

Bakke Graduate University provided the platform for me to grasp and understand and appreciate my personal-transformation journey, past and present. I quickly learned that BGU is a culture of servant leaders and change agents. BGU provides innovative and creative theological education and training for the urban Christian leader in service around the globe. Dr. Lowell Bakke helped me shape a different set of lenses and create language to articulate an urban vision of hope for myself, vulnerable children, and other least and last of society. Lowell met me at the Sea-Tac Airport. He has such an endearing pastor's heart. He is a man of joyful ordered steps. I perceived he sensed my anxiety of stepping into this unfamiliar environment and culture of Anglo servants. He phoned me just as I was deboarding the plane to say he was at curbside. After arriving at his home and meeting his wife, Diana, we had a light meal together. I had brought along hand-spa products to share with his wife Diana.

Let me give a little background on why I keep hand spa products with me. At birth my second oldest granddaughter was diagnosed with Sickle Cell Anemia/SS. This terrible affliction has sent my granddaughter in and out of ER and long hospital stays from excruciating pain crises. Blood transfusions and IVs are a few ways use to flush out the sickling cells (along with drug protocols), to give opportunity for oxygenated healthy cells to form and strengthen her body. At birth the doctors informed the parents to keep heated products available for Tyra as a way to help her self-manage the pain at home. Within a few months after my granddaughter's birth, my mother passed away suddenly from congestive heart failure. These two life and death events sent me in some deep soul searching for what God was up to in my life.

During what seemed like a long season of famine, especially concerning my sporadic and inconsistent income streams, I decided to enroll in an evening cosmetology course to become a licensed manicurist. My thoughts were, certainly I could generate a cash flow to help myself out. However, midway through my course completion Holy Spirit revealed my training would soon serve as a segue to fuel my ministry of helps calling, especially unto those who were helping professionals. Thus, after completing 900 hours of training, the business ministry of Sole to Soul Foot washing and Hand spa was formed. Seeking and securing self-heating hand and foot spa products became a distinctive in service to my granddaughter in particular, and others in general. When traveling, it was normal for me to bring a few of my products to offer to those who extend hospitality to me. In kindness, Diana Bakke was served with an aromatherapy hand spa. This was my reciprocal act of kindness to Lowell and his wife for extending hands of grace and mercy to see me into my first BGU course. Including providing me with a safe and warm place of overnight comfort.

The next day, Lowell drove me farther north to meet up with Wes Johnson in Everett, Washington. Professor Wes and Kathryn were waiting. Greetings and salutations were made, then Wes and I took off for Cedar Springs, Washington. Now I must say every step toward and into the Bakke culture was taking me further and further away from any sense of familiar and comfort. (My inner-child dialogue was fully engaged in mapping out an escape route, just in case I had to make a run for it.) Clearly this was the Lord's doing. He was creating a new extended family that would shower me with much grace and show me other ways God's Spirit would meet me and fill and restore my hope and confidence in Him.

Thank God for Dr. Wes Johnson's comprehensive, strategic, and practical BGU doctoral dissertation. In 2010, he gingerly led the contemplative coursework like it was a deep-sea (emotional) recovery effort of precious artifacts. Never had I experienced Holy Scripture in such a personal and intimate and deep abiding way. The God of the Old Testament was meeting me in my soul's deepest need in the context of the Old Testament and the New Testament. BGU was offering some pretty radical teaching on personal and community transformation. When I think on the various spiritual disciplines that were introduced to me as best practices for busy people living in urban settings, my soul cry out, "Thank you, Lord, for saving me."

Come Away and Be Still

Through the spiritual disciplines of Lectio Divina and breath-prayer exercises, I experienced renewal in ways that brought eternal satisfaction and everlasting gratitude. I was brought to tears as the spiritual disciplines cuddled me up to the face of El Roi—the God who sees me. Over the next five days, in the gentle and capable hands of Prof. Wes Johnson, I would find myself surrendering my deep ache to the One who comprehended and loved me the most. In this setting, I felt a strong sense of safety to give myself permission to be seen, heard, and thus healed.

Lectio Divina: Urban Practices

The retreat center was well-groomed, serene, and full of vibrant nature. It was a servant leader's haven. Cedar Springs Retreat Center became my place of restoration and renewal. For surely, I must have looked like the rag, tag, and downtrodden. After all, I was over sixty, unemployed, emotionally exhausted, and financially empty. Much reflection, journaling took place in this quiet, secluded place. Professor Wes was full of joy and happy anticipation as he began unpacking his thoughtfully researched dissertation titled "Experiencing God's Transforming Presence: Praying His Names in the High Points and Low Points of Life." He would use his document as a way to use scripture and the names of God to draw me closer, closer still to El Roi, the Living One who sees me. Yes, I became acutely aware of the love and protection the Living One keeps over my life.

After Dr. Wes completed introductions, he jumped right into the first exercise and teaching on the practice of Lectio Divina. Included in the binder were definitions and comments and scholarship by expert thought leaders, past and present, on the subject of lectio divina. In one handout, he shares "The goal of lectio divina is to experience the presence of the Lord through the written text of Scripture. Our goal is to pray back God's intent as he expressed it through his Spirit in the words of the text."

Psalm 131 was typed out. He moved the group through the sacred reading of Scripture. Four readings were completed. The first reading focused on a key phrase that resonated within. The second reading focused on the overall meaning of the passage. The third reading, we were asked to pray the intention of the passage back to the Lord. In the fourth reading, discover one key word that summarizes God's intention for you in this section of scripture. After each reading, instructions were to spend up to five minutes in silent meditation, reflecting on key ideas. Then, after the fourth reading you were asked to sit quietly for ten minutes in His presence, using the key word to focus your thoughts. Lastly, as a way to strengthen one's faith and testimony, you were to spend some time journaling, recording your thoughts.

Throughout the rest of the day, and the next four days, using various scriptures, Dr. Wes presented, weaved, and engaged participants in the practice of Lectio Divina, combined with the healing power of Breath Prayer, and learning how to select and pray the names of God in the high points and low points of one's life experiences. A way of connecting God's character, God's mission, and our souls deep need in our situations. One name that ministered to me then, and continues to encourage me today, is the name El Roi as revealed in life story of Hagar in the book of Genesis 16:1-6. God sees us when we are far from home; he meets us where we are and gives us a future and a hope. Like Hagar, I too, a single mother, experienced being alone and fearful. Her story became my story. God's way of showing me he was and is my present help, then and now.

During this time of reading scripture and journaling, the Holy Spirit met me in the recall of a childhood sexual violence. In one of our lesson sessions, I ask Dr. Wes if he was aware and could he handle an inner healing moment that was emerging in my soul. He reassured me that it was common to have past hurtful remembrances to arise. He affirmed that the process and practice of contemplative prayer methods was another way, and viable resource to assist one in inviting and allowing Holy Spirit in to minister to an emotionally upsetting memory. He was right. As I sat with scripture, allowing the lesson of lectio divina, breath prayer, and applying the name of God to enter into my fragile and damaged soul, I experienced an amazing inner healing transformation. How radical is that!

In my observation, one of the most conventional ways others are encouraged to address and confront painful past memories is usually conducted through formal therapeutic practices. While this helping method is a good one, for some it can take years before one can realize positive and lasting results.

Professor Wes's incredible dissertation topic proved to be a spiritual road map for me to rediscover and experience God's love in some awesome and amazing ways. Every word from the pages of his dissertation was a challenge of trusting God to change me—to transform me through praying the names of God in the high points and low points of my life. Coming to know God more intimately by his character and name moved my mindset from a skewed view of God to a dimension of love and acceptance in the Beloved. This prayer method stirred within me a lovely place of intimacy with Abba.

The contemplative prayer disciplines of Lectio Divina, breath prayer, and timelines began flowing through my soul like an intravenous bag of life-giving fluids. I absorbed every word and practice, a feeding tube for my soul. I encountered God in ways that surprised me and caused me to let my defenses down. I was trusting God in this process to handle me with care and to bring celebration to my spirit. Change was happening right in the moment—right before my eyes.

Contemplative prayer methods as spiritual disciplines and practice in my busy urban context, fortified my mental health and my spiritual well-being tremendously and impacted those in my personal circle as well. Prior to learning new spiritual disciplines, I was extremely haughty and full of self-effort. I had relied on my strength to solve problem and organize my life. I was often seen as controlling, mean, and not easy to get along with. Today in my current roles, I pause and whisper, "I trust you, Jesus." When unscheduled callers are at my door, I pause and reflect on "matters too great for me" (Ps 131). When I take a moment before responding, I inhale and whisper a breath prayer. Peace that flows like a river fills my body, mind, and spirit.

In 1996 I was introduced to the ministry of inner healing and deliverance through the extraordinary compassion, pastoral care and skill of Juanda L. Green, M.Div/LMFT, founder of New Visions Christian fellowship church in Los Angeles, CA. Her called ministry is anchored in Luke 4:18, where Jesus declares that He is uniquely anointed to bring healing to the broken places in people's hearts, to set captives free, and to lead prisoners into liberty. Through laying on of hands in prayer, along with scriptural declarations a participant may experience immediate or long-term relief from their soul's discomfort. For a short season I was placed in Juanda's pastoral Christian counseling care. She later referred me to Duncan Steele, a licensed therapist. His use of visualization as a key component in his therapeutic paradigm put me in touch with the root source of my anger. For years I held my parents (and myself) emotionally hostage. Why? Unforgiveness. My parent's inability or neglect (from work exhaustion) to protect me from the violence that came upon me as a young girl. Just months before my mother passed away Holy Spirit led me to go to my mother and ask her to forgive me.

In comparison, and from my personal experience, lectio divina puts the ownness of inner healing and deliverance directly on the transforming power of one sitting in His Presence, permitting scripture to read your soul, and allowing the Trinity to covenant you in a deep restorative process. The practice of contemplative prayer methods provides one with immediate and sustaining access to the loving care of Abba-God the Father, Jehovah Raphe-my Healer, and El Roi-the Living One who sees me. These are eternal gains. I am grateful and thankful to God for showering me with his amazing grace and mercy. Strengthening me with courage to repent and to forgive those who I had ought with (living or deceased).

Reflections

Contemplative prayer methods are timeless and true. Dr. Wes's course outline: Reflective Prayer for Transformational Leaders did more than explore key disciplines. We were asked to identify core needs in our personal lives, in both past and present situations, as a way to become our own living transformation labs. Participants were instructed on ways to immerse those needs in the character of God through: Lectio Divina, breath prayer, and praying the names of God in the high points and low points of one's life. A most satisfying and sustaining way to experience God's living presence on a daily basis.

I was ramped up and excited to report back to my Personal Learning Community of what I had learned and how I received deep inner healing from these timeless disciplines, and to share and test these spiritual disciplines in my urban context. It was my assignment to create and design a few lectio divina sessions with my busy urban leader friends. Creative ideas began flowing through me like a river.

My instructions from Dr. Wes were to allow the process to settle in within my soul. Continue to pray my breath prayer and lectio texts for an extended time. Allow self to go deeper still by praying over my personal time line. In doing so, this would keep me fortified in the spirit and in my faith as I prepared to widen my scope to introduce others to the contemplative prayer methods. I was to reflect on the question, "How might I see myself serving others with these prayer tools? Below are a few ways the Spirit prompted me to get going.

1. Titus 2 Women: An early evening session was planned. Five mature African American, servant leader women were invited to my home. These are the women who said "yes and amen" to go, learn and return to us, and teach us too. They were my personal learning community. Ages 45-69. They were thanked for praying for me. Then I introduced the project theme: Lectio Divina for busy urban leaders. the term Lectio Divina was defined and its historical significance discussed. The process began with sharing what contemplative prayer methods are, its theological foundations, praying the Scriptures (the practice of Lectio Divina) and breath prayer. After which we began the four readings of Psalm 131. In this context and time constraints, the process was shortened. Time did not permit going deeper still with breath prayer. However, participants did have opportunity to reflect and journal, and give feedback. Four out of the five women expressed a connection of intimacy with the Holy Spirit and wanted another session. Believe this process of getting still and secure in God's presence in this way is so needed and necessary for people living and serving in urban settings. One participant shared she had diffi-

cult time getting quiet. And did not get an understanding of the process. Over time she shared how practicing sitting with Scripture in the quiet of her home brought her better understanding.

2. Church Leadership Retreat: A group of ten plus of mostly African American women and few men were invited to attend the leader's retreat. Scheduled for early morning, at a social room in a condominium complex in Del Mar, CA. A brief introduction to reflective prayer for transformation leaders was shared. Several small groups were formed. Instructions were given in written form for each group to get started. group readers were appointed to set the tone with leaders, transition to small group lectio and journaling; including a reader on breath prayer. We began with four readings from Psalm 131. The facilitator encouraged and cautioned participants to be prepared for tears, uneasiness, joy, new mercy and more to emerge. Towards concluding the process of contemplative prayer methods time was spent in worship songs and holy communion. At the end of the day, participants were asked to reflect on going forward, how they will give themselves aways so Christ is seen, known, and glorified in someone's life?

3. Urban Monks. The term, urban monks is a combination of ancient and contemporary realities. Inspired by the place and space of my ministry calling to serve and advocate for young people. Thus, urban South Los Angeles would be the place to test the ancient practices of contemplative prayer. The cultural space would be a small local church of New Visions Christian Fellowship. A space where innovative gifts of the Spirit flow freely. During a Sunday worship four young African American boys between the ages of six and twelve gladly volunteered to participate in my urban monk's initiative. A patio outside the sanctuary was the place of reflection. While the method of lectio divina was maintained with four readings, followed by meditation and response, popular rap artist lyrics were used to begin.

The lyrics of a rap artist was used as a bridge to biblical themes in the music. A scripture verse (John 3:16) pointed participants focus to the person of Christ as the ultimate urban monk. The One who is their Savior and Lord and Abba Father in their urban lifestyles. The One who comforts and intercedes for them when they become frightened or anxious in the sometimes chaotic and unstable culture of South Los Angeles, CA. Each boy was then asked to pray over our time together. Feedback from each child was positive. They wanted to spend more time in the future engaging Gods word in this creative way.

4. Lectio Visioning Session by Skype: My goddaughter, Antonia Jackson, is a phenomenal social justice activist in Oakland, CA. She is a creative out-of-the-box thinker. Always open to new ideas and ways to reach the mind of young people. She and Amy were co-directors in a cutting-edge youth development collaborative in the Bay area. Both were at turning points in their professional roles. Antonia was aware of my graduate coursework in Reflective Prayer for Transformation Leaders. She called to ask if the process of lectio divina could be used to facilitate a visioning session to help them discern what the next steps in their future work together, or not. A date and time, including Skype access was established. Each were sent background on the process of Lectio divina. Psalm 131 served as the framework to get their hearts and minds ready to encounter the Presence of God in this unique way. A copy of their vision statement was sent to me. After reading and meditating on Psalm 131, we transitioned to reading the vision statement. The process of Lectio Divina was adapted to use the vision statement to engage in the four-part readings, spending 3 minutes meditating after each segment: 1) make note of key phrase, 2) focus on overall meaning of vision statement, 3). Silently pray the intention of the vision statement, 4) sit quietly in God's presence and focus on a single word. Afterwards, each participant was jour-

naled, reflected on insights, transformation and more. For these two professionals, the resolve came quickly. Within a few days feedback from one indicated her calling was moving in a new direction. One of marriage and family.

Before the transforming grace of Lectio Divina-reflective prayer practices, I lived by self-effort and driven by the propaganda of "no justice, no peace." Problem with this attitude and lifestyle, I rarely encountered or experienced inner peace, let alone any personal justice.

It would be the thoughtful servant leadership of Dr. Wes Johnson who the Lord used to help set this captive free. Once the purpose and practice of Lectio Divina was presented and caught hold to my fast-beating heart, a divine love overtook my wounded soul, and parts of my unrenewed mind. Never thought I could experience the Presence of God in such a unique way. The timeless spiritual disciplines of contemplative prayer methods, challenged me to not only face my painful past, but most importantly to learn new ways of being in God's Presence.

A profound transforming biblical story came to life before me right off the pages of Genesis 16. Selecting a name of God put me in touch with the life events of Hagar—a single mother, on the run, in the desert, with her son. Much like my life—a single mother on the run from an aching past, into an unknown place, with her young son. It was in this moment that I found my story in the Bible. In verse seven Scripture reads, "The angel of the Lord found her by a spring of water in the wilderness..." Then in verse thirteen, Hagar named the Lord who spoke to her, El Roi—the Living One who sees me. He really sees me. In what seemed to be a place of desolation and potential famine in the wilderness became a place of redemption and restoration for Hagar and for me too. The process of engaging contemplative prayer methods reconnected me to the One who sees me when I am far from home. In this instance, I felt so affirmed and accepted in the Beloved. Ephesians 1:5-7 best illuminates His love for his daughter.

"Having predestined us to adoption as sons by Jesus Christ to Himself, according to the good pleasure of His will, to the praise of the glory of His grace, by which He made us accepted in the Beloved. In Him we have redemption through His blood, the forgiveness of sins, according to the riches of His grace." Eph. 1:5–7 (NLT)

More of His redeeming love would flow from the contemplative prayer process. Dr. Wes spoke of allowing the spiritual disciplines to teach me to practice mastery over my soul. During my evening journaling, I began to weep. These concepts, disciplines and proven practices were watering my soul to overflow. I would later learn and hold fast to another one of his profound comments, "Through contemplative prayer methods, one can actually sit with God who has moved heaven and earth to be with me." How Radical is that!

Dedicated to Dr. Wes and Kathy Johnson

Chapter 10

The Practice of Radical Servant Leadership

> Service is the rent we pay for the privilege
> of living on this earth.
>
> —Shirley Chisholm

She screamed in agony and called out, "Mama Lo, Jesus said he would heal me! When is he going to help me?" Sickle cell anemia was wreaking havoc on my granddaughter's body and mind. At birth, Tyra was diagnosed with this debilitating blood disease that brings on excruciating pain crises. It shows up mostly among African Americans.

A Radical Grandmother

God pours a mighty love into the heart of a grandmother. Our God will take a grandmother's knotted human heart, and refashion it with a constant flow of grace, unspeakable joy, with a very attentive listening ear, for the sake of her grandkids. It is our God who sets the solitary in families (Psa. 68:6). At my first meeting of my oldest granddaughter, my heart melted (and melded to hers) as she embraced me in my new role. She affectionately named me Mamalo. No longer was I without a family to love on, kiss on and dote over.

But I had grandkids who loved me too. The incredible transforming power of a grandmother's love can best be appreciated in the lyrics by Holly Near:

> "Send in a thousand grandmothers
> They will surely volunteer
> With their ancient wisdom flowing
> They will lend a loving ear
> First, they'll form a loving circle
> Around the wounded wing
> Then contain the brutal beast of war
> Sweet freedom songs they'll sing
>
> A lullaby much stronger
> Than bombs and threats to kill
> A force unlike we've ever seen
> Will break the murder's will
> To the prisons we'll invite them
> The most violent men will weep
> When 1000 women hold them strong
> And pray their souls to keep…
> Let them rock the few who steal the most
> And rule with youthful charm
> So they'll see the damage that they do
> And will fall into grandma's arms
> Two thousand loving arms
>
> If you think these women are too soft
> To face the world at hand
> Then you've never known the power of love
> And you fail to understand
> An old woman holds a powerful force
> When she no longer needs to please
> She can cut your shallow life to bits
> And bring you to your knees
> We best get down on our knees

And pray for a thousand grandmothers
Will you please come volunteer?
No longer tucked deep out of sight
Will you bring your power here?
Will you bring your power here!

A word of gratitude about my only son, Frank L. Watkins. He is a radical servant of God, as father of three precious souls, and radical first responder to all their calls for support and when in a crisis. We talk openly about the cultural and family separation hardship he experienced at the age of eight when we relocated to Los Angeles. In a recent chat regarding the completion of this book, I asked what factors help shape his fortitude and faith as a father. For surely, I cannot take any credit for his winning faith that shines brilliantly as a responsible and up close and dependable father to his children. He remembers early childhood promises his father failed to honor. He said he had a vision of being a father long before he married, and he vowed that the one thing he would be to his children is being present. I was wowed by his statement. He had envisioned his role and presence in the life of children well before they were a seed in their mother's womb. How profound is that! Now that's pretty radical parenting!

It generally brings a smile and a familial connection to each one of us. My three grandchildren call me Mama Lo. Kayla, Tyra, and Frankie's love are special and invigorating to my soul. It is a love like no other. Although we are nearly four hundred miles apart, modern telephone technology allows me to FaceTime and visually connect with them.

My first grandchild was five years old when we met. Shakayla (Kaylaboo) is now a beautiful twenty-nine-year-old. Her spirit is full of compassion. Her thoughtful leadership skills emerged when we first met. She actually asked me what I wanted them to call me. I rattled off a few Nana's or Nannie, but she said, "Oh no, let us call you Mama Lo." She is bright and very creative, with a sparkling light coming through her eyes. She has a high learning curve for problem solving and analysis. She even helped her mother pass a math test. She is long-suffering and patient too. She is serving in the U.S. Navy—as my Navygirl. Her service to America makes me proud.

My second grandchild is Tyra (Tyraboo). Tyra is twenty-three years old and tenacious. The Lord deepened my servant's heart as grandmother when Tyra was born in 1999—another beautiful and bright mind. She has superb language skills. At birth, the doctors diagnosed her with sickle cell Anemia. I believed then as I continue to trust God today for Tyra's complete healing and restoration. She bounces back with incredible tenacity and drive to live, love, and laugh. When the crisis is under control and over, she engages fully in her teenage life. In 2017, between several hospital stays, she graduated from high school with a 3.92 GPA. She searches job constantly and is hired, even if it is for a short term. She has worked in sales with several companies like Walmart, Target, and Starbucks. I ramped up plenty frequent flyer rewards with Southwest Airlines during Tyra's first fifteen years of life.

Frankie is my fantastic third grandchild. At fourteen, Frankie is very aware with a gift for engaging others in thoughtful and detailed dialogue on many levels. He is joyful and grateful and seizes the moment to try new things. At eight, he became the captain of his little league basketball team. As his big sister Kayla says, "He makes my heart happy." He has a bright light in his eyes. He is astutely aware of his environment. He has strong intellectual and social skills and can engage adults in healthy discussion on many subjects. He has a heart of compassion. At seven (2014), during one of my grandma visits, I had the privilege of leading my grandson to accept Jesus Christ as his Lord and Savior. At the writing of this chapter, my son sent me a picture of Frankie praying for his sister in the hospital. He is my warrior prince! Radical love.

When Tyra was born, it became real clear to me that all my efforts at saving the world would shift and focus on being a source of support in presence and deed to the heart and souls of my grandchildren. The practice of servant leadership, as defined and lived out in the Bakke culture, would strengthen my inner woman to become aware that I was serving God as I engaged my grandchildren in the most unique and, at times, emotionally painful ways. My calling was to be present in the lives of my grandchildren. It meant ensuring they were introduced to and learned of Jesus Christ. It meant when visiting, getting them up, driving them to Sunday school, or sharing in play, board games, that always led to character-development conversations in Christ.

Even though the parents were experiencing great division and were later divorced, my role was to keep making the presence of the Lord known by showing up as often as I was prompted by the Holy Spirit. Usually it would be three to five times a year. These times were mostly when Tyra would be hospitalized for more than two days. At home, when pain medicines would not break the sickling crises, her dad (my son) would drive her twenty miles or so to Oakland Kaiser Hospital Pediatrics Unit. The nurses and doctors know Tyra well and lavish her with joyful and warm smiles when she is admitted. They have tracked her adolescent/teen life from hospital visits to doctors' visits, blood transfusions, and other life-sustaining interventions. Thank you, Kaiser Hospital—a radical hospital team of servants.

At nineteen, Tyra can now take herself and be seen in adult care at Kaiser Hospital Oakland. Tyra has declared her college major to become a pediatric nurse. It was her heartfelt expression that nurses were more attuned, attentive, and engaged with the young patient in sickle-cell pain crises. This grandmother stands wholeheartedly behind her aspirations.

Auntie Lo

Auntielo, a name acquainted with radical social justice servant leadership, advocating for vulnerable children and families in my local and global community context. The name was birthed in the children's ministry of First Berean Christian Church in Los Angeles in 1984. When I was introducing myself to two young children age two to four, I quickly discovered their challenge at speaking in three-plus syllables. After several failed attempts at sounding, shaping, and demonstrating how to say my full name, we resolved and coined the name Auntie Lo. It had a rhythmic and familial embrace for children and their families. Thirty-plus years later, the name Auntie Lo has become my servant's heart calling card. The name Auntie Lo gives me access to the souls of hurting children and families, even adults who need a touch from the Father to hear and know their lives matter to God.

Today the name Auntie Lo is synonymous with incarnational and servant leadership, showing up in the lives of hurting and helpless people—just like Jesus—up close and personal, advancing the kingdom of God in every aspect of my life, and promoting the Gospel of Peace of Jesus Christ to be known in the hearts of young children in particular. When I hear my name called out to the grandmother spirit of Mama Lo or to the community advocate of Auntie Lo, I take note of it as a summons from heaven to stand ready and draw closer to God. Be still and listen.

Children's Prayer Initiative

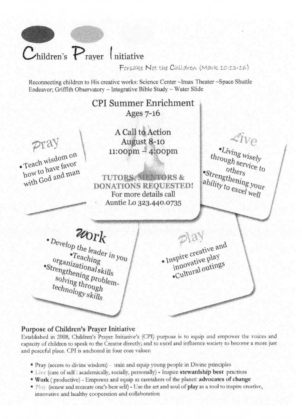

Children's Prayer Initiative

Forsake Not the Children (Mark 10:13-16)

Reconnecting children to His creative works: Science Center ~Imax Theater ~Space Shuttle Endeavor; Griffith Observatory ~ Integrative Bible Study ~ Water Slide

CPI Summer Enrichment
Ages 7-16

A Call to Action
August 8-10
11:00pm – 4:00pm

TUTORS, MENTORS &
DONATIONS REQUESTED!
For more details call
Auntie Lo 323.440.0735

Pray
• Teach wisdom on how to have favor with God and man

Live
•Living wisely through service to others
•Strengthening your ability to excel well

Work
• Develop the leader in you
•Teaching organizational skills
•Strengthening problem-solving through technology skills

Play
• Inspire creative and innovative play
•Cultural outings

Purpose of Children's Prayer Initiative
Established in 2008, Children's Prayer Initiative's (CPI) purpose is to equip and empower the voices and capacity of children to speak to the Creator directly; and to excel and influence society to become a more just and peaceful place. CPI is anchored in four core values:

* Pray (access to divine wisdom) – train and equip young people in Divine principles
* Live (care of self : academically, socially, personally) - Inspire **stewardship best** practices
* **Work** (productive) - Empower and equip as caretakers of the planet: **advocates of change**
* Play (renew and recreate one's best self) - Use the art and soul of **play** as a tool to inspire creative, innovative and healthy cooperation and collaboration

Immediately following my return home from a mission's trip in Chennai, India in 2008, the Holy Spirit summons me to mobilize and organize children around the need and effort to teach children to pray and speak to God directly. My pastor friend Dr. Velma Union opened her church to the call of community. With little resources and local help, over thirty families responded. South Los Angeles children and families laid hands and hearts to the wall of prayer. Children needed to make a connection to God. Their hearts were hurting and burdened by the parental disappointments that did not ensure housing, food, and safety measures were in place. CPI was launched under the inspiration of the Holy Spirit. And developed from the prayer model of the Royal Kids Ministry in Chennai, India.

Its purpose: teach my children to pray to me directly. Empower children to speak to the hearts of men to change society from a place of violence to a place of peace. Annual summer CPI events take place in South Los Angeles since 2008.

For the first time, my inner dialogue became settled and grounded in the healing and transforming perspectives of transformational leadership and combined the spiritual disciplines of contemplative prayer methods. I began to see that my entire essence, my calling, is to serve God first in all the fullness and strength he has endowed me in advancing the kingdom of God for the sake of the children.

It was the thoughtful, deliberate, and practical brilliance of Dr. Grace Barnes that gently guided my intellectual capital and guided imagery of what servant leadership is and can become in urban and corporate settings, including within family systems. The practice of servant leadership retooled my mindset to consider the transforming power and value of anchoring my service to God, family, and community in the concept of servant first. It was under Prof. Grace Barnes's mentor leadership that introduced me to the profound thought leader Robert K. Greenleaf.

> The servant-leader is servant first... It begins with the natural feeling that one wants to serve, to serve first. The leader-first and servant first are two extreme types. Between them are shadings and blends that are part of the infinite variety of human nature." (Robert K. Greenleaf)

In his book *Servant as Leader*, Greenleaf identifies a servant leader as "one who is a seeker, listener, one who is able to withdraw and reorient oneself...accepting, tolerant of imperfection, having a sense of the unknowable, intuitive, live by faith...disturbers and awakeners, healers...creating dangerously...and are fully human..."

The above quote from Greenleaf gave me food for thought. It gave me a way to focus that empowered my thinking to serve in a renewed way. I pondered Greenleaf's insight and sized up the characteristics of servant first to the qualities of many leadership assessment tools I've used in my leadership discovery journey. Greenleaf's insight is much deeper and lasting and relate closely to the fruits of the Spirit. However, there is a downside to this incredible knowing. One can know, discern with exceptional insight, yet encounter rejection and exclusion among one's peers. What I ascertain is, these gifts must be soaked in humility and trust in Jesus as the Master Change Agent.

In learning of Greenleaf's profound transformational-leadership wisdom, I paid close attention to his thoughts on being a change agent and a thought leader and having a presence on the boards of organizations where changes in policy and reform were needed. Greenleaf believed that boardrooms were a mission ground too. So don't run from the boardroom. Get among them and influence change from within the system. Since then, I lend my servant leadership in service to God and humanity on boards of directors, advisory groups, and committees with gladness, knowing my presence and input matter at the highest and grassroots levels of organization.

With the growing cases within the foster care system, I became curious about why were so many children being separated from their birth parents. I began to make inquiries with friends and colleagues in social services. Where are mothers? Mothers were noticeably missing from the fabric of community life. What was happening to the mothers of children being placed in foster care systems. Reports of substance abuse/child abuse (even death by misuse) of young and young adult mothers would provide me with some insight. Children were being exposed to many incidences of physical injury and sexual violence at the hands of irresponsible adults/guardians. On any given day there are over 437,000 foster care cases in the U.S., over 60,000 foster care cases in California and nearly 100 times a day a child is placed in foster care, with other 33,000 cases in Los Angeles County. https://www.clccal.org/resources/foster-care-facts/

What was God asking of me? What aspect of my heart/character was being called upon?

It was the bold and fearless servant leaders I encountered at the Christian Community Development and Advocacy (CCDA) conference in Chicago, Illinois, on September 2010. CCDA is a radical approach to community development and transformation. Like Jesus, CCDA inspires one to establish relationships among the widows and orphans then move into the neighborhood. It is the testimony of John Perkins, founder of CCDA, that drew me in closer to this association of radical believers who served in their callings in the context of incarnational leadership. They all believed it was important to live and love where you work and work and love where you live—move into the neighborhood, move into the hearts of the people Jesus love.

Bakke Graduate University CCDA coursework helped fan the flame of conception of the called and transforming prayer and advocacy ministry of When 1000 Grandmothers Pray, a monthly gathering of grandmothers and other urban leaders who advocate in prayer and show up in the marketplace to covenant over the souls of vulnerable children and families in a local, national, and global context. Dr. Nancy Murphy, a bodacious servant leader pressed me to give myself away with intention to the cry needs of oppressed children. Her lifework among First Nation people on reservations awakened me to some pretty innovative social welfare programmatic strategies.

A query with Dr. Lowell Bakke of Bakke Graduate University concerning my purpose at the CCDA conference brought a full expression of his visionary capacity, joyful inspiration, and spiritual discernment as he affirmed what he saw as my social-justice calling to the poor and oppressed. He expressed that he observed me sitting in the lobby when a perfect stranger approached me and asked me to pray for him. Without hesitation, I clasped my hands with his hands and began to pray over this young man. Lowell's encouragement to me was to remain true to what I am called to do, and that is to pray for children.

Initially, I did not see prayer as a separate entity of any transformation effort. My thoughts were each one of us is called to pray. Now to take a prayer strategy and give it life would be a major challenge. I had no idea how to launch such a ministry, but I did believe it would be a different model than the conventional prayer meetings happening in local churches on a typical Wednesday noon or evening. God would have to create an opportunity for me to establish a viable urban community transformation expression, so I waited and listened.

After the CCDA conference, my charge was to return to my neighborhood and create a community social justice and advocacy outreach response to the concerns of vulnerable children. It would take several months of contemplation and waiting before the Holy Spirit would reveal how I was to get started. Female pastors of non-denominational churches are unique and sensitive to the moods of its congregants.

During a worship service at The Lord's Church at 91st and Western Avenue in South Los Angeles, Dr. Velma Union shifted her message to attend to the seeming downtrodden spirit of one of her members. The size of the congregation was less than twenty-five people. The atmosphere was warm and Familia. Pastor Velma engaged the grandmother with a few questions of why her soul was so low. The grandmother stood and expressed deep concern for her grandson. Pastor Velma asked if she wanted prayer. In that moment, I exclaimed in a whisper, "That's it, when grandmothers pray!" Nine months later, When 1000 Grandmother's Pray Prayer Advocacy became a living organism. In that instance and context, the name of the prayer ministry was formed and solidified. I exclaimed out loud, "That's it! When grandmothers pray!"

Purposeful Life of Grandmothers

A GATHERING OF WOMEN INTERCEEDING FOR
CHILDREN—JEREMIAH 9:17, MARK 10:13–16

In October 2011, when 1000 Grandmothers Pray Prayer Advocacy Initiative took on physical life. What was just an idea, a thought, now was becoming flesh—muscle and sinew. "Shall these dry bones live…?" (Ez 37:6). Within nine months, October 2011, Dr. Velma Union, pastor of The Lord's Church (TLC), partnered with me and my local church, New Visions Christian Fellowship, and hosted the grand first gathering at the Lord's Church. Over one hundred invitations were mailed out. On that day, October 2011, the heavens opened and poured rain like never before. Seven people showed up. The Spirit confirmed that seven was sufficient to launch, lead, and move heaven on behalf of vulnerable children. This prayer ministry would not be for the fainthearted. Large crowds would be a distraction.

Now in its eleventh year, When 1000 Grandmothers Pray Prayer Advocacy Initiative is organized with the express purpose to mobilize and strengthen the prophetic voices of grandmothers and urban leaders to seek peace for the city and covenant vulnerable children in prayer. It is a social justice response to the number of girls witnessed being prostituted in my neighborhood along Western Avenue in Los Angeles as well as the growing number of girls being seduced into human sex trafficking and thousands of girls and boys being placed in foster care.

The Whites' House in Fresno

The Whites' house in Fresno, California, is without alarms, guard dogs, security, and pretense. It is incarnational leadership at its finest. In fact, a stranger is apt to receive just as hearty a welcome as an expected guest. My plane had been delayed by an hour. Randy's wife was there to pick me up. When I arrived at the Whites' home, the multinational student comrades were present in full force. Nations of Africans and African Americans and Anglos and other unnamed people groups occupied Randy's home for dinner and to participate in our first lecture and instruction on what it meant to be engaged in a city immersion program of Bakke Graduate University Global Leadership Program (a discipline of hope). Great care, coordination, and patience went into ensuring that each student had accommodations in the homes of residents or neighborhood hotel/motel rooms in walking distance to the Whites' home.

In the context of shalom leadership, believers are mandated to "seek peace and the welfare of the city to which I have caused you to be carried away captive. And pray to the Lord for it" (Jer 29:7). There was a shift in my thinking after hearing, learning, and receiving the mandate to pray for my city. My early church experiences did not teach me that believers were to pray for their cities as expressed in the book of Jeremiah. Protest for social justice put the burden of responsibility on local and national government to take action. Now I see it is my personal calling to pray for my city and expect the organized church to give voice for the voiceless and oppressed too.

LORETTA B. RANDLE, M.A.

The Chingangu's: From Africa with Love

Three weeks prior to attending BGU City Immersion in Fresno, CA., October 2013, my home was host to servant leaders, Bishop Teddy and Pastor Lister Chingangu of God Our Help Ministries, Int'l, Zambia, Africa. I met Lister in 2008 at a small lunch gathering of women pastors in Encino, CA. She had been invited to the United States by World Vision, International and selected to speak before Congress in an appeal for international aid to help with the HIV/ Aids pandemic in Zambia, Africa. Former First Lady, Laura Bush hosted her visit. Jeff Witten, Account Executive, of World Vision International made the initial introductions.

Each morning at the rising of the sun, Teddy and Lister could be found praying prostrate on the bedroom floor in my home in two or three different languages: Bantu, Swahili and maybe a heavenly language. My home would be rocking and reeling from a very strong prayer language. All I could do was to hold on to the side of my bed and pray in my feeble prayer language. The Chingangu's message was simple and clear to African Americans in particular, "You are our Joseph. Forgive us for selling you into slavery." Will you teach us how to fish? Will you teach us how to become self-sufficient? What a powerful demonstration of their love and reliance on God to carry such a heavy message from Africa to America. Holy Spirit strengthened me and compelled me to connect them to friends and neighbors and local churches with their message of reconciliation. Five churches (over 50 plus friends) were impacted by the faith and holy boldness of this couple as they would lay prostrate for mercy and forgiveness. Each time they would engage in this public display of humility, my soul (and others) would cry out, too. Something deep on the inside was being set free. Two days prior to my flight to Fresno, I drove Teddy and Lister to LAX for their return journey back to Africa. The Chingangu's showed us what incarnational and servant leadership looks like from a global perspective. At this writing both Teddy (2014) and Lister (2021) Chingangu have transitioned into the presence of our Lord and Savior Jesus Christ. Daughter Charity Chingangu has stepped up to continue the good work God has begun in God Our Help Ministries, Int'l. Local churches, friends and neighbors stay connected in prayer and resources to help sustain the outreach efforts of the ministry.

New Visions Christian Fellowship Church

What began as a Friday night worship-and-praise gathering in 1991 has today become an organized church of believers trained in the biblical models of creative and expressive worship practices using flags, banners, prophetic singing, lyrical dancing and more, all with emphasis on bringing inner healing and deliverance through worship. In its early formation and development, the founding pastor, Juanda L. Green, would facilitate praise-and-prayer gatherings in her Los Angeles apartment. This worship ministry model and calling are birthed in the biblical context of Isaiah 61:1–4: "The Spirit of the Lord God is upon me, because the Lord has anointed me and qualified me to preach the Gospel of good tidings to the meek, the poor, and afflicted; He has sent me to bind up and heal the bro-kenhearted…" Worship and praise are orchestrated in intentionally selected lyrical audio music. In this environment, the climate is set for the listener's heart to rest and receive comfort and restoration in the arms of God, accompanied by laying on of hands and prophetic prayer whispers of Jesus's love in the ears of individuals. Trained ministers stand ready to receive the full weight of the individuals in their arms as they surrender to the weight of His glory.

It is in this creative and liberating worship and praise setting where I received Christ in my life as Lord. He had been my Savior since the age of twelve, but I never allowed Jesus access or surrendered all the damaged places where anger, bitterness, and unforgiveness had created much entanglement and barriers to my heart. It would be in these praise and worship and prayer settings where I could openly cry out my hurts and disappointments among leaders who would hold me in their embrace and rock me in the cradle as though I was in the loving arms of the Father. In these settings, I found myself asking God to forgive me for holding my parents, siblings, friends, and systems in captivity for the early childhood hurts and violence heaped on me.

Learning to worship the Lord openly, loudly, and unashamedly began setting me free from a life of animosity and rebellion. In this atmosphere, the compassion of the pastoral care and counseling team began experiencing an increase and observance and hearing of per-sonal-transformation testimonies and changes. It was during these times of weighted worship moments where my heart for missions, local and foreign, awakened to the call to "go ye therefore…" and began to grow deeper and wider to extend help to vulnerable children and families. The more the Holy Spirit was given freedom to move in and on my desolate soul, the more I began to experience freedom to see, hear, and articulate my dreams and visions for the sake of empowering children as change agents. Now that's a radical worship model!

My professional development travels with Citizen Ambassador Program, to the former Soviet Union, Ukraine, and Kiev, were insightful and personally rewarding. Our tour guides were well informed of the 1500-year antiquity of tradition, customs, and social-political norms of their country. We met, and had roundtable discussions with women who managed farms to women who supervised the production of watchmaking. Women were being placed and promoted in leadership and management roles in various industries. It had been just three years prior (1989) that the Berlin Wall came tumbling down. Yet, here I was among a nation(s) in transition (1992). As bold as I present myself to be, being this far away from home, in a foreign land, became a little unsettling.

It would be a visit to a memorial park in Ukraine where the Lord met me in a special way. In this place, a few of my group participants deboarded and walked around the periphery of the park in solemn memory of their ancestors who had been persecuted and killed and buried at the hands of Nazi leaders. This was sacred ground. I became still, quiet on the inside and respectful of the souls who took time to remember their love ones. Then I thought of the trials and tribulations of Africans and the devastation of American slavery. All those who did not make the Middle Passage, and those who arrived, only to face some fierce persecutions, lynching's, beatings and murders, and destruction too. Similar to the despicable treatment and death of the ancestry of Ukrainian people that is happening in 2022. Now, back on the tour bus, some of my Anglo sisters returned teary-eyed and grievous. Prompted by the Holy Spirit I began to engage a few of the women in gentle talk. They shared family memories. It was then we became a closer, tighter network of women leaders from America. Looking back, I can see how God was shaping and forming my servants' heart by revealing and removing my prejudices too.

Time away in the former Soviet Union did not create a welcome mat to my return-to-work life at United Way, Inc. in Los Angeles. The climate was tense and unstable. New leadership was dismantling my employment security. Within weeks I would be engaged in a fierce wrongful termination lawsuit. Again, unemployment benefits became my source of income. My local church affiliation was in a battle for new leadership. I found myself visiting other churches. I was asked to help form a new church organization with new leadership. Still in search of where the Caller was leading me. So in 1995 I found myself on a mission's trip to Johannesburg, South Africa with a team of twelve mission-hearted souls, with loads of products. During this season of what seemed like a never-ending spiritual battle and income famine, I cried out to God a lot. Where did I fit? Throughout these seasons of transitions, I volunteered with several charitable and nonprofit organizations.

I thought I was ready to serve on the global stage. Not so. There was still much more preparation work necessary before I could think about serving in a worldwide organization. In 2001 I was hired by World Vision US Programs as manager of children and family's initiative—a unique and innovative youth outreach program named: Visions Youth Initiative. It was in this context where my global Christian outreach training and grounding would be perfected. My sense of servant hood would expand greatly in this missions-oriented culture.

God was planting seeds of servant leadership along my life's journey. In early 2003, during a World Vision online development video, I was attentive to a young girl about the age of twelve who made an appeal to World Vision global leaders at a conference in India. Her appeal had much to do with calling the adults out of their comfort. She said, "Try living my life. Walk in my shoes of poverty and voicelessness." Until this day, her passionate message of advocacy remains in a sacred place in my heart. Her message and appeal inspire me to live and love the children of India too.

Manhattan Beach Pier had become my waterfront office where I would go to listen for God's voice and instructions on what's next for me. My employment with World Vision US had termed out (December 2007) after seven good learning and development years. World Vision enriched my professional-ministry capacity greatly, equivalent of a master's level education and training in corporate servant leadership and innovative child advocacy. A good model of a global servant organization. Who knew, within a few months I would be inflight to Chennai, India.

Gazing at the ebb and flow of the waves moving ever so carefully to the shoreline, then out again into the massive expanse of the ocean. Curious, I asked God, what's on the other side of the horizon? After several hours of ocean therapy, I drove home and sorted through the mail. I opened a letter from John Robb, (former) Director, Global Prayer Mobilization of World Vision International, and chair of an organized network of Children in Prayer (CIP) movement (now International Prayer Connect). It was a formal invitation to join with other like-minded adults in a time of prayer, consultation and reflection regarding ways to mobilize, teach and train the next generation of youth prayer workers and leaders.

Forty nations gathered in seclusion in Chennai, India, and discussed and prayed—forgave and prayed for each nation—and visited the Royal Children's Ministry under the visionary leadership of Father Antone. It was during a foot-washing ceremony of inducting children labeled "untouchables" into the school when my heart seared and burned to advocate even more for the sake of children. After my return to the United States, Holy Spirit filled me with inspiration to form and set in place the outreach ministry of Children's Prayer Initiative Los Angeles.

A year later, John Robb invited the outreach ministry of Children's Prayer Initiative in Los Angeles to collaborate with the 2009 United Nations Ambassadors Prayer Initiative sponsored by Concerts of Prayer in cooperation with several innovative and creative national and international prayer movements. John Robb, CIP, invited me and my team to join this prayer endeavor. Over five hundred global intercessors converged on Manhattan, New York. Two delegates from my local church context were anointed and prayed over and released to go.

Laura L. Gordon and I were trained and licensed as ministers of the Gospel of Peace in 2002. We were trained under the apostolic and prophetic leadership of Pastor Juanda L. Green. Laura, founder and CEO of a boutique business management firm Gordon and Associates, and Gammy's House philanthropic organization. Laura and I have spent many years in creative and innovative prayer gatherings and community engagements, serving in missions-oriented service projects, locally and globally that directly impact vulnerable children. Her heart to develop a strategic mission to undergird her business-charity endeavors led her to Kings Seminary. At the time my mission's calling and development was under way through several national and global service organizations. But could benefit from some sound theological doctrine to strengthen my foundation. Led to Fuller Theological Seminary in Pasadena, CA., I enrolled in the school of Psychology, Family Life Education, with an emphasis on developing a focus in Christian formation for children. A few years later I would be immersed in the servant leader and learning culture of World Vision—a global Christian Community Development and Child Advocacy global organization with a presence in 100 countries. Being a part of a state-of-the-art mission's culture of servant leaders proved a more creative way and spiritually enriching in advancing the Kingdom of God.

My cumulative mission's endeavors are fueled by my called servant work experience in the culture of World Vision, Inc. In the WV context, my ministry development outreach capacity expanded in national and global urban contexts. Life after World Vision led me on a mission-oriented Christian travel to Chennai, India, in 2008.

New Visions Community Development Initiative

After my 2015 BGU graduate degree completion celebration, and filled with Christian community building strategies, I went into high gear and established a community development initiative, framed in TL perspectives, within my local church. When 1000 Grandmother's Pray Prayer Advocacy, a radical outreach arm of New Visions Christian Fellowship. It permits participation at civic events and community-based collaborations that focus on the health and wellbeing of vulnerable families and children, particularly black infant maternal mortality. Girls Club of Los Angeles, a 50 year child and community development resource agency, became our supportive and credible strategic stakeholder, and wise counselor, as we entered into social justice networks and funding streams in the public marketplace. A sampling of marketplace community engagements of New Visions Community Development Initiative:

1. Project: BestStart4B Black Babies: a collaboration of grassroots organizations and capacity building partnership with institutional support of First5LA, Community Health Councils and other significant stakeholders and South Los Angeles African American Infant Maternal Mortality Community Action Team (AAIMM/CAT). (2019)

2. Project: Phone H.O.M.E.: Helping Others Manage Emergencies—in collaboration with Los Angeles County Department of Mental Health: a community-based approach to addressing the mental health and well-being of children, older adults and veterans in Los Angeles. In partnership with creative and healing arts professionals—healing drum circles for women, faith-based lyrical movement demonstrations, and healing sounds of nature percussions, participants were informed and trained in ways to ground and center in the spirit of Shalom. (2018).

3. Project: HAPPI: Healthy Aging Partnerships in Prevention Initiative: a research driven health and wellness collaboration with UCLA Center for Health and Data Research, T.H.E. Health and Wellness Centers, and older adults at risk of colon cancer. An information and education outreach model created and delivered in seminar format as a way to increase one's awareness of home-based colorectal screenings among African American and Latina women and men over the age of fifty-five (2017).

4. When 1000 Grandmother's Pray Prayer Advocacy. A local and global network of older adults called to seek peace for our cities. Purpose: mobilize and strengthen the prophetic voices of grandmothers and urban leaders to covenant vulnerable children and families with prayer, and in presence. (2011).

Reflections

In this chapter, Practice of a Radical Servant Leader—before the term servant leader entered my perspective, the spirit of servant had begun shaping and forming my son and I in some pretty radical and innovative ways. At age eight my son rode the waves of change that were set before us as we left small town Vallejo, CA, to metropolitan Los Angeles, CA. We were surrounded by and with courage and boldness to step into unfamiliar places, among unknown people. God's grace and mercy were surely our supports. Frank adapted quickly to lots of new people, and new places. He did so with grace, charm and peace. He stayed ready to support his mother when the winds of change shifted with either people or our locations. Looking back, I can see how the Holy Spirit was forming and shaping his inner man too. He has an incredible compassionate soul. A servant father to his children and a son's presence of strength to his father. You see, my son, grands and grandpa all live together back in Vallejo, CA, serving one another in grace and mercy.

Let me acknowledge the extreme radical love the Lord deposits in the heart of a grandmother. The word radical suggests a return to its origins, its root. My take is the Lord is restoring the joy of family that was first experienced in the Garden of Eden, before the Fall. As for this radical grandmother, a love so strong has returned me to my roots in God original intent for humanity to love one another freely, pray unconditionally, live joyfully and give thanks gloriously. A radical grandmother stands ready—to go the extra mile. To jump on a plane to sleep at the foot of a grandchild's hospital bed. To take a 400-mile road trip to be present at her grandson's school for grandparents' day. To stay on my knees for the safety and protection of a granddaughter away serving in the Navy.

Moreover, this same Love so strong, places me (Auntielo) in submission and obedience to God to be present in the lives of vulnerable children through various child advocacy networks. Such as establishing the called equipping ministry of Children's Prayer Initiative and When 1000 Grandmother's Pray Prayer Advocacy Initiative. Including keeping my heart and home open to domestic and foreign missions and missionaries too. Training and development are key to listening to the voice of God, and learning innovative ways to share the love of Christ to vulnerable and urban children. An excellent urban city community development and transformation example was experienced at the White's house during a BGU Fresno Immersion. Observing the care and practice of servant leadership in action, through the person of Dr. Randy White, as he opened his home, teaches and demonstrates on the value of exegeting one's neighborhood, then to walk it out in such humility was watching God at work in the flesh.

It is hope that each of you are practicing the love of serving in your unique way. If you haven't already, invite the Holy Spirit in to heal and deliver you from your painful past. I write as a living example of how our Lord (if you let Him) took my dark sinful past and transformed and renewed a right spirit within me through the practice of contemplative prayer methods. He has placed my life in the marvelous light of redemption, restoration, and renewal, changed this once broken-in-spirit single mother, and made her into a bold and courageous grandmother. A useful vessel of honor as servant of the King of Kings, for the sake of the children. The practice of servant leadership is a call to action to all people, older mature adults, and grands in particular. Servant leadership is an intentional act of obedience to the One who loves you. The One who moves all of heaven and earth to be with you. He knows your name.

Dedicated to Grandmotherless Children
(Royal Children's Ministry in Chennai, India and
God Our Help Ministry in Lusaka, Zambia)

Chapter 11

A Call to Action: A More Compassionate Theology of Children

Forsake not the children…

—Mark 10:13–16

A picture hangs on the wall of my home office, labeled, Visions of Our Future. Multiethnic faces of several children dressed in diverse cultural clothes shine the light on the hopeful faces and opportunities children are to look forward to. Yet, African American infants and children remain objects of deprivation due to continuing historical racial disparities.

The bible mandates believers to not forsake the children. (Mk. 10:13-16). Thus far, violence against infants and children continue to prevail. Since 2018 the outreach ministry of When 1000 Grandmother's Pray Prayer Advocacy have extended covenant partnership with Los Angeles County Public Health: African American Infant Maternal Mortality movement to join our voices with other child advocates for the sake of the survival of children (Prov. 31:8-9). Calling heaven to strengthen humanities compassion to elevate awareness and change the trajectory of black babies not living beyond the first year. Research confirms that systemic racism plays a strong part in ignoring and or attempting to place the burden of blame on the mother (blackinfantandfamilies.org). A call to action of a more compassionate theology of children is needed to honor God and to bless his children: "Lo, children are a heritage of the Lord: and the fruit of the womb is his reward (Psa. 127:3).

Transformational Leadership Skills
for the Twenty-First Century

"Transforming urban cities from places of darkness and decay to places of hope and new life involves new leadership skills," says Dr. Randy White of Center for Transformational Leadership in Fresno, California. In 2013, White charged Bakke graduate students to define transformational leadership for their personal and ministry context. My inspired definition of TL is, "submission to the incarnational calling of the servant leader to seek Shalom for the city. TL is informed by intentionality and authentic faith in action through significant people called to strategic places. TL is inquiry, engagement, and reflection into the pain and hope of people and places. TL acts as a catalyst in the formation, nurture, and strengthening of social-spiritual infrastructures, along with the mobilization of neighborhood-based networks that effect signs (disciplines) of hope on a personal, community, and systems level." Overall, TL is a calling to encourage individuals, public or private servants, in discovering the best in people for the sake of the kingdom of God.

Skills for the twenty-first century should definitely include a viable and necessary prayer component to usher in healing and lasting change to people, places and spaces. Adding contemplative prayer methods as an essential TL skill is crucial to the health and sustaining well-being of any attempt at change. As a helping professional and Christian spiritual coach, a course in Reflective Prayer for Transformation Leaders surely would undergird the efforts of making lasting changes that can heal. Applying the principles and protocols of contemplative prayer to my personal circumstances set me aflame with a new life centered deeper in the love of Christ. I'm convinced that these prayer methods can further enrich the expertise of those in servant leader role—whether child or adult. Benefits abound to the interior of the souls to those who seek to cooperate with children and families in the transformation of their city and families at becoming places and spaces of Shalom, where nothing is missing or broken.

As agents of transformation, When 1000 Grandmothers Pray Prayer Advocacy Initiative seeks to connect with, strengthen, and partner with existing community networks that make up the spiritual-social infrastructures that are charged with caring for children.

Eight Perspectives on Transformational Leadership

The collaborative effort of When 1000 Grandmothers Pray integrates its core values in the context of the global community transformation movements as presented by Bakke Graduate University's eight transformational leadership perspectives. These perspectives provide the framework for formalizing and expanding the prayer ministry of grandmothers and urban leaders into a community collaborative network. TL is informed by eight core values that act as a catalyst in the formation of social-spiritual infrastructures. TL is inquiry, engagement, and reflection into the pain and hope of people and places. Calling-based leadership, incarnational leadership, and servant leadership perspectives provide anchors that inspire the vision and purpose of When 1000 Grandmothers Pray Prayer Advocacy Initiative.

Calling-based leadership is founded on the premise that there is a Caller. It is a personal, inward call of the heart. I believe it was in Fresno where I heard it said that "Transformational leadership is about stewardship of power." That power of great influence and incredible responsibility was witnessed through the called lives of Father Abraham and Sarah, Moses, Joseph, Samuel, King David, Nehemiah, and Queen Esther. Each one had the opportunity to misuse and abuse the power God had given them, yet they stayed the course and fulfilled their portion of the Great Commission.

In the spirit of calling-based leadership, in book of Gen. 21:2 of the Bible, Sara conceives and gives birth at the old age of ninety. So, am I called at seventy plus—daughter of 1960s, a least and unlikely servant leader grandmother—to seek to understand her God-given gifts, experiences, and opportunities in her unique role as a called instrument of Christ's transforming work for the sake of the children living in vulnerable and hard urban settings.

When I reflect on the story of Jesus engaging the woman at the well, this becomes a model for urban leaders to use to understand incarnational leadership (Jn 4:6). Here we see Jesus showing urban leaders how to pursue and share in the experiences and plights and hopes, including sharing the knowledge and work of transformation. Mother Teresa's life exemplified incarnational leadership in a most profound way. She copied the self-emptying act of the Word becoming flesh as specific strategies of community transformation in behalf of children. Then many urban leaders consider the story of Jesus laying aside his garments to wash the disciples' feet as the ultimate example of incarnational ministry (Jn 13:12–14).

In the same example, Jesus Christ shows me how to become an even more sensitive and attentive servant leader as I seek to serve urban leaders. As the ministry of When 1000 Grandmothers Pray seeks to expand outside its comfort zone and become a more vibrant collaborator of community connectors, I understand my behavior and priority are on servanthood first—that is to say leading by serving and serving by leading. Servant leadership values the importance of asking, "What are you called to do in the position you hold, and what could I do or be to help you fulfill that calling? In this context, the heart of Christ is incarnated in the role of servant leader. Among the grandmothers and urban leaders, there is a strong and living presence of service.

Grandmothers show up faithfully at Faith Children's Development Center in South Los Angeles as volunteer foster grandparents and to offer extra hands in the classroom with teachers and in the outdoor play areas. A grandmother is quick to stand for social justice too. When 1000 Grandmothers Pray Initiative marched along Western Avenue in solidarity with civic, government officials and others to give voice to the voiceless and reprimand perpetrators that our children are not for sale in the evil child-sex-trafficking wickedness. "Reflective leadership calls for the urban leader to live in reality, reflect on its meaning, and catalyze others with the courage, symbols, and example to make meaning in their own lives." Grandmothers marched with boldness and confidence.

Contextual-leadership perspective is related to that of incarnational leadership. Both are intentionally focused on external expressions of the gospel in transforming community. One exception, however, is that in CL, except the "leader goes deeper and wider by recognizing the previous work of God in other cultures and seeks to experience its unique gospel expression." The Lord provides an exceptional exchange of contextual leadership and culture right in my home and in my neighborhood. Contextual leadership bridges the TL perspective of global leadership in a most unique way.

The history of my neighborhood is couched in two cultures. My home was built in the early 1920s. Local church edifices show signs of earlier Anglo-American settlers. Up until a few years ago, remnants of their presence would show up in annual visits of aging white Christian men in their mobile homes for cross-culture exchange at a local United Methodist Church in my neighborhood. Today my neighborhood consists of an aging population of African American homeowners and new Hispanic family dwellers.

Ancient history and a community's relationship to the larger city, state, nation and globe should look at and consider the role and impact that sociopolitical, economic, religious, and other influences have played in shaping and affecting a place and space. TL perspectives of incarnational, global, prophetic, shalom, and servant leadership played out when the Lord sent two thoughtful and compassionate missionaries to my home in 2013. For nearly a month my heart would witness, change, weep and connect to the souls of these two courageous believers in Jesus Christ.

My observations, these two witnesses of Jesus Christ clearly were called and aligned and disciplined in the Gospel of Salvation. Their allegiance to Jesus Christ was unmovable. For three weeks the global city of Lusaka, Zambia was present and sitting in my living room in Los Angeles, CA. It was in this context of hosting God's sent ones that the Lord made a sweet connection with my global African heritage and my African American experience to my national American history.

They responded to the Caller. The Chingangu's were on a mission. From Africa to America. The message was clear and twofold: reconciliation with brothers and sisters in America, and help Zambia live again by teaching them how to fish. They used the life story of Joseph in the Bible as a basis for their appeal for forgiveness for selling African Americans into slavery. Accompanying them from church to church and neighbor after neighbor, Teddy and Lister extended brotherly love in profound and demonstrative ways as they stretched out on the floor in humble submission before the people. Hearts were being mended and healing took place after each encounter. Teddy showed much compassion as he spoke Truth with love through the power of the Holy Spirit. My militant mindset was shifting again. Peace flowing like a river began to flow with ease and tenderness through my veins.

These two global sent ones modeled TL leadership perspectives in unique and consistent ways. Prayers of Shalom covered me and my home, and destitute hearts living in and among my neighborhood of the City of Los Angeles. At sunrise, morning by morning, laying prostrate on the floor of the bedroom, prayers flowed and filled my home in multiple languages: English, Zambian tribal dialect, including their heavenly language. In love they came. In love we sent them back to Zambia, not only with full hearts, but resources to strengthen the outreach efforts of God Our Help Ministries, International—

help to the widows and orphans impacted by the HIV/Aids pandemic in the land.

As I reflect on the theme of this chapter: A Call to Action: A More Compassionate Theology of Children I give God the glory for sending living examples of faith in response to the Caller. With just airfare, Bishop Teddy and Pastor Lister arrived at my home from Lusaka, Zambia, Africa. Without a budget, the Lord opened the eyes of my heart to extend hospitality to these missionaries. For three weeks food, clothing and transportation and more flowed daily to care for God's precious vessels.

On a global front, the church at large is seemingly engaged in strategies of community transformation for the sake of children. There are faith-based networks that show themselves compassionate on national television. Then there are local churches that are doing good things for poor people—food banks, skid-row outreach, shelters for the homeless, and so much more.

Yet children seem to be more at risk than ever before. On a global front, two hundred girls were abducted from a local school by Islamic terrorists in Kenya. Some say nearly three thousand children are seduced into prostitution in the United States on a daily basis. However, we believe the prophetic prayers of grandmothers, touching the heart of God to move on the hearts of men, to snatch our children from the hands of the enemy and play a key role in this accomplishment. A June 2014 news report announced a successful sting operation that rescued over one hundred children from a child-sex-trafficking ring. The grandmothers rejoiced.

Global partnerships and prophetic prayers are on the radar screen of When 1000 Grandmothers Pray Prayer Advocacy Initiative. We are in covenant prayer with God Our Help Ministries International in Lusaka, Zambia, in Africa; International Prayer Connect; Children in Prayer International; and USA-Zambia Development Council located in Los Angeles, California.

Our goal is to connect our prayers (and resources) with Zambia's prayers to move on the hearts of men to get immediate relief to the widows and orphans. Further, the prophetic prayers of grandmothers are in agreement with the United Nations Millennium Development

Goals to end poverty and hunger, have access to universal primary education for children, attain healthy lives for all, and have available and sustainable use of clean water. These are just a few of the goals we are in agreement with for change and transformation for all children.

The grand's collaboration (seven Ps) has expanded its transformation prayer reach by targeting academically low-performing and highly behavioral-challenged schools, especially pre-K and local elementary. We do so as a strategy to spiritually dismantle the unjust criminal justice system's intentional "pipeline to prison" phenomenon. If an African American child is not reading by third grade, by age nine, business decisions are made to build new prisons with this target group in mind.

A more compassionate theology of children is rightly stated. Having a biblical foundation to understand God's heart for children and by which to exegete my city has been an incredible transforming learning curve. So much so that God picks children from among the families of faith throughout the line of Abraham to fulfill his mission of redemption of all creation and restore sweet communion to all those who call on the name of Jesus—beginning with Isaac and his boys Esau and Jacob on to the twelve boys of Israel, including Joseph and his sons, followed by baby Moses to King David and the climactic birth of our Lord and Savior baby Jesus. We then can see and witness the prominent theme and status and value of children throughout the Bible.

God's rebuilding plans are more than a notion. I have learned that any community-transformation effort must begin with prayer. Thus, the transformational prayer ministry of When 1000 Grandmothers Pray stands much wiser, stronger, and better as agent of change. In addition, contemplative prayer methods are strongly suggested to include in the transformation leadership tool kit, an essential skill to the helping professional, parent, educator, pastor/priest, including law enforcement, in the sustaining work of Christian community development and advocacy.

BGU Fresno immersion coursework provided me with a discipline of hope in the structure and models of transformation to glean from and adapt to my local and global context. One example is expanding the ministry to become a community collaboration that is connected to the seven Ps of community engagement of parent, principal, pastor/priest, police, politician, and physician, combined with the prophetic prayers of grandmothers and other urban leaders.

Intentional and strategic prayer as a viable strategy toward community transformation bubbled up while in a learning/teaching intensive in 2013 led by God's anointed leaders Dr. Randy White, Dr. Lowell Bakke, and my student comrades from different global locations. My vision of transforming my city is poised to bring the light and love of Jesus Christ in and among my sisters and brothers in the faith but mostly to children who are living in hard places and who wish to know they have a Father in heaven who cares for them.

All children matter to God. We have aligned our prayer efforts with the Millennium Development Goals to end poverty and hunger, to raise women and children up from their sickbeds. Most importantly, we are to seek ways and discover opportunities to inform others about the love of Jesus Christ in the setting of the cities to which we are sent. If one child in the world lacks protection and provision, then all children are at risk of the same. So we pray, "Thy kingdom come on earth as it is in heaven...give us this day our daily bread... but deliver us from the evil one..." (Mt 6:9–13).

A call to action is the inspiration of this chapter. Today, children are seemingly still the scapegoat for many of humanity's social ills. Children living in and out of home care, separated from their birth parents, now come under the custody of the Department of Children and Family Services throughout the United States. "Nearly one hundred times a day, a child in California is placed in foster care. Los Angeles County alone "parents" over 33,000 abused and neglected youth in foster care." https://www.clccal.org/resources/foster-care-facts/

Moreover, studies consistently report that a high percent of child sex-trafficking victims have been involved in the child welfare system. Children are precious in God's sight. "Behold, children are a heritage from the Lord, the fruit of the womb is a reward" (Ps. 127:3).

To my older-adult friends, grandmothers and grandfathers, childcare workers and other child advocates, stand your ground in the spirit of righteousness and justice in the marketplace. Our children need you, warrior prince/princesses. Believe that your life matters even more so at sixty, seventy, eighty, and beyond. If you have breath in your body, say a prayer for a vulnerable child. If God can give Sarah strength to conceive and give birth at the age of ninety, then surely he can breathe a breath a prayer in you for the sake of a child in need.

The Spirit of God is still at work within this seventy-plus daughter of God! Living and serving urbanites in Los Angeles, especially from my home, at times can become overwhelming and mentally taxing. Recently, I invited two young men, both in their early twenties, from my neighborhood to chat with me (while they mowed my lawn) about their plans for the future. To help me understand better the mindset of why young men their ages are not asserting themselves to get where they want to be in life. Their responses were vague. Neither one is in college, they work at odd jobs, and live at home with parents. I reached out to a clinician friend who counsels young people, African American males in particular. In our chat, he referenced and shared that many young men and women in this age group are experiencing anxiety and depression. They are failing to move forward into adulthood. Social scientist and therapist refer to this behavior as failure to launch syndrome. A call to action is clear. Afterwards I was inspired to pray and ask the Lord for ways to help this young population discover their purpose. A focus group with a few retired educators and justice workers concur that not only is a behavior intervention needed, but a grandmother's presence in the lives of young people, would add great help also.

According to a report by AARP, by 2030, older adults will become the largest people group in America. In AARP Livable Communities Initiative, it projects that "by 2035, there will be more people over the age of 65 in the United States than under 18." I laid my hands on some old notes from another provocative BGU course, Kingdom Story Retelling. My notes capture how God chooses and makes the least and most unlikely people into His servants who make a difference. Surely, I wrote these notes from my perspective of being counted out and dismissed in various circumstances in my life. Course after course within the BGU context helped me discover my story in the Bible story of redemption and servant leadership.

Over and over again, Old Testament key features of God's plan of redemption were brought to pass through the most unlikely people with hearts of submission: aging Abraham and barren Sarah, baby Moses floating on the Nile into the hands of Pharaohs daughter; hated and imprisoned Joseph. Moving forward in history we can see how the hand of God moves on two destitute widows: Naomi and Ruth—who would later become grandparents to King David—who began as a teen shepherd boy. In the New Testament, in an unlikely turn of events the Holy Spirit shrouds Mary, a young teen virgin girl from the ghetto of Nazareth, to become the mother of Jesus. Children and young people matter to God.

In addition, older adults are one of the most underutilized transformation resources in the Church and community. They are societies least and most unlikely people. But He will use them to accomplish His will in the redemption efforts to change the trajectory of young people's hearts from darkness and despair, towards a life of flourishing.

This is an urgent call to action. A call to the hearts of grandmothers, helping professionals, educators, community-based organizations, faith-based organizations, including institutions that have a solemn obligation to care for young people, and to all who have an ear to hear. These community stakeholders and others are creating a think tank to share ideas and strategies that could reasonably complement existing work to at risk youth with personal leadership development skills. One organization that stands out as a beacon of light with a mindset of community action is the compassionate servant leadership of Girls Club LA. A 50-year-old community-based organization that began as social justice response to the early education needs of underserved, low-income families without access to affordable childcare. Today it stands as a diverse intergenerational model of a nonprofit corporate servant leader. My call to serve children is within this organization in partnership with Pepperdine University-Foster Grandparent Program, as a volunteer servant leader.

Chapter dedicated to Girls Club LA
Pepperdine University Foster Grandparent Program
DreamCatcher Foundation Residential for Girls

Chapter 12

Finishing Well

Well done my good and faithful servant...
—Matthew 25:21

Knowing God and having confidence that there is a plan
and purpose for our lives should fill us with euphoria. As I
am awakened to a brand-new day, I am grateful to connect
with my Divine calling as a sovereign voice of authority on
assignment in the earth... I become elated and joyful.
—(Author Unknown)

My local church hosts summer movies on the fourth Sunday of each
month beginning July through September. An outreach strategy
attempt to invite neighbors and friends and gather family generations together to watch, listen, and learn how God shows up in ordi-
nary lives on a daily basis in extraordinary ways. The church selected
the movie, *Same Kind of Different as Me*. A film based on a true story
about an unlikely friendship between a homeless man and a wealthy
art dealer, unfaithfulness and the transformative power of love, mercy
and healing. During these Sunday movie offerings, it was customary to push pause to allow others to reflect, ask questions, and give
feedback. Surprisingly, an eight-year-old girl casually approached the
microphone and said, "What I got from the movie is it doesn't matter
how you start, it's how you finish." Well, needless to say, all the adults

in the room were awestruck by her profound insight. I was deeply moved by her confidence and sense of surety of the words that flowed from her mouth. Surely the Lord had spoken. I followed her to her seat and hugged and kissed her all over her face, with whispers in her ear that her life matters to God and to me.

What does an eight-year-old know? Obviously, the Lord places value on the mind, heart, and soul of an eight-year-old. From this young unlikely soul, the Lord illuminated the power and presence of Jeremiah 1:5: "Before you were formed in your mother's womb, I knew you…" I believe children are endowed by the Holy Spirit with incredible capacity to learn and to know. Children are like sponges soaking up conversations, inspiration, and motivation, including observation of the good and the ugly. In Mark 10:13–16, Jesus is found admonishing the disciples to not leave the children out:

> Then they brought little children to Him, that
> He might touch them; but the disciples rebuked
> those who brought them. But when Jesus saw it,
> He was greatly displeased and said to them, "Let
> the little children come to Me, and do not forbid
> them; for such is the kingdom of God."

Believers are to be intentional in speaking words of life, hope, and love in our encounters and connections to and with children.

Courage to finish

Courage. It can be expressed as strength in the face of danger, pain or fear. While channel surfing late one evening, I came across a teachable moment on what courage might look like when one is called out of a familiar space, and enters into a new and unaccustomed environment. In particular it focused on the process of transformation of a dragon fly. At the appointed time, it is prompted by an unknown or internal clock, emerges from its ocean floor and watery existence, and crawls upwards above water, and onto a reed. Now exposed to air—it quickly learns to breath above water in a new and different atmosphere. Courage shows up as the dragon fly must now hang from a reed, over animal infested and murky waters for *three* days while its wings become strong. Does three days symbolize the time of divine transformation? Jesus was buried for *three* days. On the third day he arose from the dead. Discarded his grave clothes and ascended to heaven. Back to the dragon fly, in the presence of potential risks and difficulties and despite the danger, hangs in there for three days until its change is complete. Then it takes flight.

It took big nerves to begin and end this book writing effort. Courage was absolutely necessary. At times I was not sure if God would leave me hanging alone. Or if in fact, when I needed breath, if he would strengthen my fragile soul. I cried out for constant reassurance to open the eyes of my heart to know His love was present and would not fail me in this endeavor. Chapter after chapter, fear and anxiety would team up to dissuade me, as untold stories of hidden violence and neglect were being revealed and recorded. Yet, as the Angels ministered to Jesus after 40 days in the desert, Holy Spirit refreshed my soul with living waters of affirming words of friends, weekly meals, including drives to the ocean for self-care. Yes, I questioned if I had what it takes to write and to do so in command of the English language. Structuring words and grammar are not my strong suit. It would be a hit and miss in this body of work. But thank God for technology to spell check, grammar check along the way. A quote on writing by Ray Bradbury caused me to consider writing from perspective instead of apprehension and fear: "Your intuition knows what to write, so get out of your way." So, I spoke, I am a writer, a writer is what I am.

For 100 days I was engaged in intentional, daily prayer, meditation with Holy Spirit. These contemplative disciplines became my steadfast source of inspiration to keep the faith, and with courage let the life of Christ speak to and through me as an instrument of His transforming peace. Lectio Divina would set me up for fellowship with Jesus and a new dimension of intimacy with my Lord. I began to look forward to meeting the Lord morning by morning on my porch in warm sweet communion. Allowing his Word to read my soul for an hour.

Unlike the dragon fly, I hesitated to step into this new space of learning to intended to breathe new life into my story of change. For I would be exposing, not only my soul, but the life of family and friends to potential judgement too. I took the risk of trusting God to bring forth my voice through processes that brought forth inner healing and character formation. Reflective prayer methods became a critical transformation asset used to inform, encourage and teach me to wait on the Lord, and believe the Word of God. "From a biblical perspective, part of being strong and of good courage means trusting in the Lord as our true source of strength" (Google.com). Giving myself permission to let my life speak through this book surely has illuminated his unfailing love. The biblical fact that it is God who breaths the heart of Christ within us to give us confidence and safety to speak our truth with power and authority to overcome our problems.

In the midst of writing, Covid 19 pandemic put a halt on the world's heartbeat and life expectancy of older adults in particular. It literally took our breath. Fears escalated, and many wondered if this would be the end of us all. Citizens were mandated to mask up, line up and test weekly. Prayers and prayer lines expanded in time and frequency to pray for the bereaved, sick and shut in, including leaders in Washington. Personal health challenges persisted. Unplanned flights to attend to my son and his family health emergencies took priority. Throughout the height of shelter in place, increased listening sessions and intercession put demands on my pastoral care calling, including my ministry partners of When 1000 Grandmother's Pray. My home became a hub to check in and gather for prayer and support to one another. Cleary the Lord was stretching and expanding our ability and faith muscle to call upon heaven to touch earth and show up and comfort the cry of the people.

Towards the end of 2021, I had become extremely exhausted and emotionally spent. Thank the Lord I felt no-shame at requesting mental health and wellness checks with my local health clinic. In addition, local food banks greatly increased their presence in more neighborhoods in South Los Angeles. Access to fresh vegetables were available to me and the grandmothers in the network, neighbors and friends on a weekly basis. Just as the Spirit of God sent the raven to feed the prophet after strenuous intercession, so he made a way to feed me also. I give thanks to God for his infinite wisdom, grace and compassion during periods of uncertainty.

Finishing well immediately offers up the idea of completion and celebration of writing my first book. Unholy events that were intended to crush my spirit became opportunities for the Holy Spirit to infuse my soul with courage to keep pressing in purpose to finish. Today, I remain hopeful as the Spirit opens the eyes of my understanding to know that finishing well is not a single event. But more of a continuous process of obedience to the Caller of divine direction, correction and instruction. Morning by morning, I was compelled to yield my spirit to new, transformed beginnings.

As I reflect on those who lived bold and bodacious public lives. I pause and give praise to the open-book, colorful and resilient life of an unlikely world influencer: Maya Angelou. My Shero. I certainly can relate to some of her trials and tribulations and painful past experiences as a young African American woman, single mother, silenced by early childhood sexual violation and other traumatic events. However, Maya Angelou's personal triumphs outshine and sparkle far greater than her past troubles—a community activist, artist, author, influencer, poet, teacher, and world-renowned ambassador of goodwill, and so much more. Love apprehended her and she flourished and finished well.

One of Maya Angelou's quotes inspire and remind me of His steadfast love that never ceases: "Love recognizes no barriers. It jumps hurdles, it leaps fences, penetrates walls to arrive at its destination full of hope." I'm overwhelmed with gratitude to know and believe that I have been the object of His affection all this time. His love pursued me then and does so now. His love apprehended me and changed my knotted human heart into a pliable, flexible and tender heart of service to children and humanity. God will take your pain and use it as preparation to perfect your divine purpose. My life is an open book for another to ask God for courage to get going with her story. My life is becoming an example of how God will use the most unlikely individual to give voice to injustices and unrighteousness.

Imagine me, called in the midst of my pain, transformed to serve as an instrument of His Peace, to advocate in global prayer cultures, for the sake of the children. Jesus is calling the least and unlikely to come and serve. Older adults and grandmothers, that would be you!

Finishing Well

The good work the Lord has begun in me is marked by legacy—leaving a record of thanksgiving during times and places where God met and delivered me from all my fears. Stories of accomplishments one leaves for family, friends, community, and generations to come. Footprints leading to a transformed character. Remembering my parents, who in the face of daily hardships, were endowed with much *courage* to fight the good fight of faith and finish the good work of serving family and humanity with all of their strength—without economic justice, health care justice and social justice my family experienced more good days than bad ones. My parents' example of a servant foot print to work while it is day lives on in my DNA.

Finishing well this writing endeavor is a major accomplishment. Although it took much longer than I had hoped for, the process of finishing well required me to submit to the Holy Spirits timeline. As I reflect on the challenges of transformation, I faced in writing this book, a quote from Palmer Parker shares the inner work that took place as I ventured forward in the face of insecurity. "We have places of fear inside of us, but we have other places as well—places with names like trust and hope and faith." These three-character strengths became my new friends. Additionally, God would send encouragement through the mail, too. AARP featured an article on the endurance and astonishing story telling of three young women survivors of human sex trafficking. Surely, I could unashamedly keep writing and revealing and telling my story of triumph too. A second story of deliverance came before me during a writing slump. An unsubscribed magazine was on my porch. An article lay opened on the outdoor table. It tells a story of a well-known person's triumph over poverty, early childhood sexual abuse, and more. I believed God was sending me messages of hope and strength to keep going with my writing.

Finishing well serves as a milestone and a navigational tool to guide others in their search of significance and identity in Christ. Knowingly leaving a historical landmark that says, God met me here. Just as God instructed the children of Israel to create a rock formation as a memorial to remember that it was God who saved and fed them while they were crossing many tumultuous plains. "Let this be *recorded* for a generation to come, so that people yet unborn may praise the Lord..." Psalm 102:18 informs the utmost importance to *write* in the spirit of leaving a legacy. Thus, giving life and meaning to a living and ongoing story of triumph, survival and flourishing, created by the shed blood of Jesus Christ. In my recollection of a 1992 visit to the former Soviet Union, landmarks and memorials were constant and present at nearly every stop we made from Moscow, Kiev and the Ukraine. Marked by signs on walls, art, carved in sidewalks, and created in sculptured statues and more. These landmarks serve as a message that life mattered in the moment and space and time, and would be remembered for generations to come.

Legacy. Keep learning. Following degree completion and celebration of my Master of Arts in Global Urban Leadership program, Professor Grace Barnes invited me to *continue learning* to perfect my skill set as a professional coach and consultant. She introduced and led me through an amazing six-week coaching engagement and visioning process called Strategic Futuring. A unique visioning process created by Ray Rood, Founder of the Genysys Group, that includes reflection, visioning, analysis, dialogue, planning and action—a directional tool to guide you toward the life you dream of creating. Strategic Futuring challenged me to envision my future up to fifteen years forward and put some legs to it. Dared me to concretize my vision of a renewed life. Another dimension of professional (and evangelistic) equipping to go into the marketplace with a tool to ground others in fulfilling their called purposes. The Lord was making some incredibly precious investments in this once damaged and broken vessel, and unlikely servant.

Reflections. 50 years ago, I was a hot mess—emotionally, physically and psychologically spent. It would take a month of Sundays of swimming around in a sea of meaninglessness, searching for love and acceptance and wanting for courage. Although much afraid, I heard the Caller say come. I left the familiarity of domestic violence as an outcast in small town Vallejo. Today, I celebrate a new life overflowing with heartwarming intimacy with my Lord. A vibrant and hopeful life of promise. Beyond three-score and ten, this seventy-plus grandmother embraces a wonderful ascended life in Christ.

In the bounty of His loving kindness, he calls a grandmother. My Lord shaped and formed a new heart of tenderness—a most unlikely in society to be a voice for the voiceless. Older adults, grandmothers in particular, matter to God. In a 2010 interview with Oprah, Jane Fonda shared her newfound love of grandchildren, "Grandchildren cause your heart to open up and expand to a new dimension of love that is unimaginable and unfathomable." Only the Spirit of God's love can do such a thing. My first encounter and experience with my oldest granddaughter warmed my heart. Then, two more grands later my heart became liquified with a love that opened once closed doors in my heart. God was using these precious vessels to prepare my heart for the Potter to reshape and mold in His image for service to the rag, tag and poor, beginning first, with me.

Who told me I could write anyway? Running away would have been my pre-transformed past behavior before immersing in something new and telling as BGU coursework—courses that not only stimulated my curiosity, affirmed my identity in Christ, but informed my story telling strengths of transformation. Oh yes, it would be my BGU professor of Servant Leadership, Dr. Grace Barnes, who lit a flame of writer within my and psyche. My transparency and openness in telling and reflecting on my story, as an open book is an example, she uses in her book writing tool kit. It would be in these liberating contexts where my deliverance from religious rules of dos and don'ts would be challenged, replaced with sound biblically based compassionate leadership thought and models. My writing efforts were fueled and framed by the inventive and innovative courses of BGU, grounded by eight transformation leadership perspectives. What I learned and know for sure is I am strengthened in my inner woman, and thrive in my understanding, integration and application of these unique, and easy to accept biblically based values; that frame my new and improved character strength and my Christian community development mindset and lifestyle. Despite my rebellious past, Lectio Divina taught me that God will leave heaven just to be with you. He will take your entangled heart and create a new one, to be sweet communion with you.

Professor Grace Barnes asked me to tell my story—visions of my transformed future. With God's grace and confidence, wisdom and skill, I write. Holy Spirit has me up to creating more imaginative ways to introduce the love of Jesus Christ in the life of children and families. It is my intent to sit before God, with hope to live long and strong to make it so. One aspect of practicing being present with children, is listening attentively to them, focused on the voice of God speaking in the child. We are to help children tell their stories too. One unique way my local church uses to get kids talking is through superhero movie Sunday. Each fourth Sunday a Marvel movie theme is selected and viewed in part. The children watch and eagerly wait to give input on different scenes. Then the facilitator shares Jesus Christ as the ultimate and final Superhero. When I am with my grandchildren, and those I refer to as my community godchildren, listening to

163

their stories of triumphs, joy and laughter, my heart smiles. Children are curious and aware. I am strengthened and encouraged to keep giving voice and advocating in places and spaces where children are voiceless—from the womb to the classroom and to the boardroom.

When I would begin to waver in my faith and belief that God is calling me, the biblical story of Sarah surfaces as a reminder and legacy of endurance in the face of great social disgrace. During her childbearing years, she waited patiently for the promise of children to manifest. But to no avail. God would surely get all the glory in this story as the Promise keeper. However, it would take all of twenty-five years to prepare the hearts of Sarah and Abraham to trust God to keep his word. So, at age ninety, a very old adult woman, with a desolate womb, is shocked into belief. God s gives Sarah the strength to conceive and give birth to her son, Isaac, the promised one. What I see and now know for sure, it is the Lord who gives us courage on the path of life. Sarah and many of my ancestors leave me with a legacy of the discipline of hope. One of trusting and waiting on the Lord— to complete in us that which he has said he would do, in His time.

When I become discouraged and despair over matters of this life, and by the world systems that attempt to silence older adults, I am quickly reminded to find steadfastness in remembrance of biblical and historical characters like Abraham and Sarah, Harriet Tubman, Mother Teresa, Rosa Parks, Maya Angelou, and many older adults, and other unsung heroes. The steps of God's called servants leave incredible memorable footprints. Visions of my future, implies legacy. I leave you with just a few of my legacy practices and insights.

Legacy. Honor, affirm and celebrate family ancestry. Remember those who blazed a trail for you, who prayed for you. Writing my first book brought excitement and elation. At other times, I did not think I would arrive at concluding this adventurous and, yet, trying writing journey. For professional writing help and tips, I read various books of bold African American female writers, including other authors who wrote about writing well. For inspiration, I called upon memory of the trials and tribulations and successes of my ancestors and parents. Even recalling my fourth-grade teacher, who introduced me to the love of words through spelling bees, stimulated me to keep moving—Encouraged, I called on the unity of the Spirit of Christ in family, friends and confidants in my community of learners. They brought laughter (some with a bottle of wine), cheered me on and affirmed my healing and achievement was nigh. Because of their support during my desert storm, they certainly deserve to dance with me in the rain of delight. I salute my family past and present. Finishing this book writing journey, and overcoming unforeseen challenges along the way, is cause for celebration, particularly for those whose footsteps created a trail for me to follow. It is an honor and privilege to leave a legacy of record by adding my story to the stories of triumph of my family ancestry.

Legacy. Choose love not fear. "For God so loved the world, that he gave his only begotten son, so that everyone that believes in him may not perish but have eternal life" John 3:16. In her book, The Gift in You, Dr. Caroline says. "When operating in your gift you are free to choose love and not fear. Christ can then use you to help others find their fit in the puzzle—their gift. This is love," says Leaf. This kind of proactive thinking was pretty profound and liberating. To know I could literally choose to ignite the practice of love as an option to my well-being opened the eyes of my understanding in a monumental way. I would learn, we have other character strengths we can elect over fear—like hope, trust, joy and peace.

Legacy. *Practice being in His Presence.* Transparency and familiarity with Christ are our highest calling. Intimacy was a radical idea. This character strength was given room to grow, space to occupy in the renewed places in my soul. I had to learn to trust God with all the broken pieces of my shattered soul. Day by day he met me in His Word. Little by little, new habits and disciplines began to form and a new normal emerged. I began devoting time to read selective Scripture aloud to begin my day. God the Father patiently waited on me as I learned to openly sit in his presence, accept and embrace his intimacy, and to entrust my whole heart to the One who showers his love unconditionally. Writing this book served as a way for me to learn to resolve my insecurities of feeling safe and secure while sitting in His presence. Contemplative prayer practices provided a firm foundation for me to encounter his mighty love.

Legacy: *Make peace with your past.* Forgiven those who have trespassed against you. For forty plus days, the Holy Spirit ministered to me in deep inner healing and deliverance of painful past memories. It would be in these moments of quiet time, allowing selective Scripture to read my soul, that I would be strengthened in my inner woman to ask God to forgive me for my unforgiving heart towards others who were responsible for causing hurtful events in previous times of my younger life. At first, I did not feel strongly about making an intentional and verbal confession out loud, but in obedience to my Lord the words, "I forgive you...," began to flow from my lips. The power of confession before heaven and earth is incredibly redeeming. Reflecting on the power of forgiveness, and making peace with one's past can lead one down the path of physical, emotional and spiritual well-being. My relationships with my son, siblings and friends, but mostly my inner woman, are greatly improved. Peace, hope and gratitude are byproducts of the act of reconciliation.

Legacy: *Advocate for injustices and keep on in faithful service:* Speak out for those who cannot speak, for the rights of all the destitute. Speak out, judge righteously, defend the rights of the poor and needy." (Prov. 31:8-9) The called ministry of When 1000 Grandmother's Pray is a social justice advocacy response to helpless children in the foster care system, child sex trafficking, and other social ills." Let your life speak in word, deed or written speech, for the sake of vulnerable children and families. Whatever you start has a chance of lasting on well beyond your participation...God will recognize and reward faithful service...make it our aim to be pleasing to him (2 Cor. 5:9-10).

Legacy. *Importance of fitness, personal leadership and self-care/love.* In this life it is essential that one engage in the practice of physical wellbeing. Pain in the body is inevitable as we age. I celebrate fifteen years of victory over cancer. The discipline of a morning and evening walk are my daily rituals and have been for over twenty-five plus years. After the cancer surgery I was invited to participate in a physical fitness research program for survivors after treatments. The program was offered by Loyola Marymount University in Los Angeles. I learned a wide range of fitness techniques to strengthen and replenish bone health. Keeping an indoor trampoline and exercise ball in my home are absolutely necessary to keep osteo at bay—by stretching my hip and back joints I am able to keep them lubricated and loose. Another physical activity that I began and fell in love with in 2018 is Salsa dancing. After learning it is a great workout for my hips, I became a fan. Whenever I hear the sound of Latin music, I get happy feet and respond in-kind (chuckle). During the Pandemic, my uptake of herbal and nutritional supplements increased three-fold, and I continue to maintain this protocol. Routine quarterly health checks with my doctor and dentist are scheduled in advance. Including, monthly mental health wellness checks. I am a lifelong learner and have a love for documentaries that focus on nature, ecology, multiculturalism, social justice, health and wellness justice, music and art that inspire healing to world cultures.

Social enrichment. Fortified by staying connected to old friends and making new acquaintances, enlivens my emotional health. One day a week my son and grandchildren make it a point to facetime or have a brief chat. During the week I meet up with friends at local coffee shops, and occasional lunch/brunch meals to inform and encourage one another.

Spiritual enrichment. My soul is nurtured by inspirational messages accessed through social media apps, personal daily devotions, and in person participation at my local church and other church sponsored activities. Including, prayer gatherings and online subject-specific enrichment courses.

Vocational enrichment. My personal leadership development involves creative and new ways to minister to others, children in particular. Teaching in the church, consulting and mentoring; and offering workshops and seminars to the community at large, using social media, are useful ways to keep the main thing the main thing: Put God first and his Kingdom work as our primary vocation and aim. A new training and development component of When 1000 Grandmothers Pray is underway. Project S.E.E.D: Strengthen, Educate, Equip and Develop the capacities of older adults to communicate and facilitate God's heart and justice for children, using technology as a source and platform to advance the message of eternal life.

Self-care/Self-love: Integrating the practice of self-care through-out my day reminds me to give thanks with a grateful heart by celebrating the completed work of the Cross. Because he arose, we who believe can now begin to make the choice to thrive and flourish. My self-care practices often take me to the ocean one day a week to reflect, journal and refresh the mind of Christ in me. Appreciating the mighty and joyful wonder of his creation refreshes my soul. Including, the practice of deep breathing throughout my day, and short walks in my neighborhood, keeps the oxygen flowing to the brain for optimum well-being. A big wellness practice is to find reason to laugh with and about something (preferably with a child) throughout your day. Laughter releases endorphins—the brains feel good chemical. It improves mood and shrinks levels of the tension causing hormone that produces cortisol. Seek to be the best version of yourself, daily. Leaving a legacy goes well beyond what you have done. But emphasizes that which continues to flourish well beyond one's lifetime. A practice of selfcare and selflove discipline are important ingredients to a well lived life. In her book, Sacred Pampering Principles, author Debrena Jackson Gandy promotes the necessity of the practice of Innercise. That is to say, "working on the Self from the inside out—taking time to reflect and contemplate tones and strengthens our spirits." The capacity to self-reflect permits one to excerpt the decent from every encounter and involvement. A necessary transformation leadership character skill to enhance on the journey.

This book writing endeavor is not only a finished well project, but at its core is a call of encouragement to action of older adults, grandparents in particular. Like Simba in the movie Lion King, you may have forgotten your called purpose. It took Rafiki to knock Simba's head with a stick to help him remember. The Holy Spirit is your Rafiki. He is your guide to help you remember you are a called instrument of Gods peace. Now it is your turn. Your time to make history and leave a noticeable and continuing influence, a permanent footprint for your children's children's, children, to follow. My hope is more stories of trial and triumph will flow from the bellies of bold and brave older adults, grandmothers and urban leaders.

He will provide you with inspiration from the perspective of the Cross. Have great expectations of the Holy Spirit. You will be endowed with power and authority you will need to get going. Rise up you beautiful and bodacious women and men. He knows your name. Jesus is calling you to open your hearts and mouth for the good of advancing Shalom for the sake of the children. The Holy Spirit will endow you with courage to set loose your tongue and pen to let your life speak for the good of others.

All my personal actions, goals, and strategies sound well and good, but what I have come to learn and know is that transformation is a process and that it takes time (and time in prayer) and commitment. At times, TL gives me a false sense of being a superwoman of change, although it has transformed the way I see myself and my role in the world. But as Dr. Randy White states in his book *Encounter God in The City*, "Transformation means the development of shalom. Shalom is best defined as making things as they ought to be for people, in people and between people." If we are to give our efforts to the transformation of the city, even as minds are being renewed, we must yoke our undertakings to the goal of seeking shalom in systems of care in our families, in churches, and in the city. Change and transformation are not easy.

My radical servant leader calling compels me to show up and be present in my volunteer and mentor role at Faith Children's Center in south Los Angeles, California. This service work—Foster Grandparent Program and Girls Club LA, a multigenerational approach to community volunteerism—is a long-standing community collaboration with Pepperdine University. My service in this program, coupled with previous incarnational outreach experiences, fuels the way I show up in the spirit of shalom for children.

Furthermore, I believe God uses one's former life and work experiences as tools of transformation. My previous professional work life as an executive director of a youth development organization and as an associate director of organization training of a corporate charitable organization, including specialized training in social justice and advocacy, provided me with the needed skills for my present-day oversight and volunteer role as a community development strategist in calling-based leadership perspective in my local church context and community engagements.

What's more, at age seventy plus, my radical servant calling keeps me fully engaged in the innovative social justice and advocacy outreach ministry of When 1000 Grandmother's Pray Prayer Advocacy. Its purpose is to mobilize and strengthen the prophetic voices of grandmothers, urban leaders, and others in covenant prayer with vulnerable children and families. It was established in 2010 as a social justice response to call heaven and earth to put a stop to the number of children being prostituted and seduced into sex trafficking, including the number of African American boys not reading by nine, thereby creating a pipeline to prison phenomenon.

The New International Version of the Bible writes in Proverbs 31:8–9, "Speak up for those who cannot speak for themselves, for the rights of all who are destitute. Speak up and judge fairly; defend the rights of the poor and needy."

This book is done. It is a call to action. Now it is your turn to make history. Tell your story. My hope is that more untold stories shall flow from the bellies of bold and brave women. Have great expectations of the Holy Spirit to endow you with power and authority you need to get going. Rise up, you beautiful and bodacious women and men. Jesus is calling you to open your mouth for the sake of all children.

I close this chapter, but not my story of transformation, with a quote from the profound wisdom of theologian, spiritual leader, and author, Dr. Howard Thurmond: "Don't ask what the world needs. Ask what makes you come alive, and go do it. Because what the world needs is people who have come alive."

Thank you for listening!

Personal Reflections Exercise

Radical Servant Leadership in Action

A quote from Rick Warren, pastor of Saddleback church: "The best time to love is now." I suggest the best way to express that love is by serving others. Now is a good time for radical servant leadership. Children and the elderly are the two most unrepresented people groups in society. Neither one has a lobbyist or any strong representation in Congress to speak of. However, Jesus is our greatest advocate, champion. Imagine the two most vulnerable persons, children and older adults, empowered and equipped with voices to change culture and the hearts of humanity. Imagine the prayers of children moving the heart of God, moving heaven to action. Now imagine the power-packed prayers of grandmother's, coupled with the hearts cry of children, touching in agreement for change and transformation. Now envision those prayers moving heaven and earth to create a more peaceful and just society for the two most defenseless citizens in our social order.

In the exercise that follows, you are being challenged by the writer of this book, Loretta B. Randle. Your instructions are to imagine yourself in a position of power, with grace and authority, and resources to usher in positive change and ongoing transformation to the world and its flawed systems of care.

With your bible and journal in hand, reflect on the three questions below. Before getting started engage in three deep mindful breathing exercise before each reflective question.

1. Why are you here? What are your passions, dreams, and hopes for a better world? Meditate on Jeremiah 1:1-5 and Psalm 139:13-14. Begin journaling. Write freely. Allow your thoughts to come to life on paper. Avoid judging.

2. What disturbs or upsets your peace? Write in your journal three social issues that directly impact the safety and wellbeing of children? Specifically, vulnerable African American children and families. After you have made your list, meditate on Proverbs 31:8-9. Reflect on this Scripture and journal your thoughts.

3. What are you doing about it? Select one of the social issues you listed above. List an organization, or create an organization where you could apply your understanding, power, authority (with grace), and resources of radical servant leadership approach in shifting the outcomes for vulnerable children and families. Meditate on Psalm 127:1-4, Mark 10:13-16 and James 1:25, 27. Reflect on these Scriptures and journal.

Some suggested ways you can show up for the sake of children:

1. Pray for children, always. Start a prayer group or prayer line specifically for at risk kids.

2. Read to/with a child. Inquire at your local library.

3. Volunteer at a local child development center. Mentor a child in foster care. Tutor.

4. Use technology to connect with children, your grandkids in particular, use Zoom, Facetime, WhatsApp and other social media to have a positive presence in the life of a child.

5. Write letters of support to your local and national legislature that advance dollars to early child education and youth development.

6. Call or write to a local community organization and thank them for their service to children and families.

7. Give, donate, pledge and/or offer financial and in-kind resources.

8. Connect with the monthly gathering of the strategic global prayer network of When 1000 Grandmother's Pray Prayer Advocacy Initiative: a social justice response to children
   a. placed in foster care,
   b. seduced into human sex trafficking,
   c. African American boys not reading by nine, including black infant mortality, and
   d. children diagnosed with childhood cancer.

Website: When 1000 Grandmothers Pray: Under construction
EMAIL: 1000grandmothers@gmail.com. and
      Newvisionscfc@yahoo.com
FB: WHEN ONE THOUSAND GRANDMOTHERS PRAY

By your works, voice and presence, let all of heaven and earth hear you declare, "Children are indeed a heritage from the Lord, the fruit of the womb a reward" (Psalm 127:3). Shalom.

References

"Loneliness among Older Adults: A National Survey of Adults 45+." Washington: AARP Research. 2010.

"Older Adults Living Longer." *AARP the Magazine* (2010). Accessed November 27, 2018. 2018.

Angelou, Maya. *The Collected Autobiographies of Maya Angelou*. New York, NY: Random House, Inc. 2004.

Bakke, Dr. Lowell. "Loretta B. Randle, Interviewed by Dr. Lowell Bakke." Los Angeles, CA. November 2009.

Bakke, Raymond J. *A Theology as Big as the City*. Downers Grove, IL: InterVarsity Press. 1997.

Bradbury, Ray. "Your Intuition Knows What to Write, So Get out of Your Way." Goodreads.com. 2018. Accessed December 9, 2018. www.goodreads.com/quotes.

"California Children's Law Center of Foster Care Facts." 2015. Accessed January 2018. CLCCAL.org/fcfacts.

Same Kind of Different as Me. Directed by Carney, Michael, 2017.

Degruy-Leary, Dr. Joy. "Post Traumatic Slave Syndrome" (Lecture). 2011. Accessed November 2018.

Greenleaf, Robert K. *Servant Leadership: A Journey into the Nature of Legitimate Power and Greatness*. New York, NY: Paulist Press. 1977.

Guzik, David. "Wisdom over Worry." Enduring Word. 2018. Accessed November 29, 2018. https://enduringword.com/bible-commentary/psalm-37:23-25/.

Initiative, AARP Livable Communities. "Preparing for an Aging Population." 2018. Accessed December 9, 2018. www.aarp.org/livable-communities.

Johnson, Dr. Wes. *Reflective Prayer for Transformational Leaders.* Bakke Graduate University. 2010.

Nouwen, Henri J. M. *Life of the Beloved: Spiritual Living in a Secular World.* New York, NY: Crossroad. 1992.

Palmer, Parker J. *Let Your Life Speak: Listening for the Voice of Vocation.* San Francisco, CA: Jossey-Bass. 2000.

Bakke Graduate University, "Eight Transformational Leadership Perspectives—Leadership Definitions." Seattle, WA. 2010.

West, Dr. Cornel. Los Angeles County 2nd District Empowerment Congress Summit. 25th Annual Empowerment Congress Summit. University of Southern California: Los Angeles County 2nd Supervisoral District. 2015.

White, Randy. *Encounter God in the City: Onramps to Personal and Community Transformation.* Downers Grove, IL: IVP Books. 2006. Table of contents only. http://www.loc.gov/catdir/toc/ecip0612/2006013027.html.

Endnotes

1   David Guzik, "Wisdom over Worry," Enduring Word, accessed November 29, 2018, 2018, https://enduringword.com/bible-commentary/psalm-37:23-25/.
2   Ibid.
3   Maya Angelou, *The Collected Autobiographies of Maya Angelou*, New York, NY: Random House Inc., 2004.

About the Author

At age sixty-seven, Loretta B. Randle, M.A., received her master of arts in global urban leadership from Bakke Graduate University, with a concentration in servant leadership. Advocate, ambassador of Christ, and author of her first book: *Reflections of a Radical Servant Leader*. The book is written with an appeal to the older adult, African-American women in particular, to pick up your cross and serve the Lord with gladness and urgency! With a compelling message to the emerging young adult that your life matters to God and in service to humanity.

She is founder of When 1000 Grandmother's Pray Prayer Advocacy and Children's Prayer Initiative, outreach ministries of New Visions Christian Fellowship church. Equipping the voices of urban children and grandmothers to communicate directly to God is at the core of her servant leadership calling. She shares her journey of personal transformation with transparency, passion, and urgency. She uses her life experiences from angry, emotionally damaged runaway African-American single mother at age twenty-five of an equally fretful eight-year-old African-American son, to becoming God's chief radical servant leader. She is a senior strategist, social entrepreneur, trainer, wellness enthusiast, writer, and urban minister. Loretta B. Randle offers innovative strategies in service on various community and faith-based boards of directors to influence positive change agenda's for the sake of the children.

On the horizon are e-Course/seminars: Know Thyself—a character strengths series to the emerging young adult and a mindful leadership lead well series master class for the helping professional. She has one amazing adult son, Frank, and three exceptional grandchildren—Shakayla, Tyra, and Frankie Jr.